# HOW MUCH IS YOUR ★VOTE★ WORTH?

A publication of the
Center for Self-Governance

# HOW MUCH IS YOUR ★VOTE★ WORTH?

## THE UNFAIRNESS ★OF CAMPAIGN★ SPENDING LIMITS

### FILIP PALDA

**ICS PRESS**

Institute for Contemporary Studies
San Francisco, CA

This book is a publication of the Center for Self-Governance, dedicated to the study of self-governing institutions. The Center is affiliated with the Institute for Contemporary Studies, a nonpartisan, nonprofit, public policy research organization. The analyses, conclusions, and opinions expressed in ICS Press publications are those of the authors and not necessarily those of the Institute or of its officers, its directors, or others associated with, or funding, its work.

Inquiries, book orders, and catalog requests should be addressed to ICS Press, 720 Market Street, San Francisco, CA 94102. (415) 981-5353. Fax (415) 986-4878. To order, call toll free in the contiguous United States: (800) 326-0263. Distributed to the trade by National Book Network, Lanham, Maryland.

The editor for this book was Jan Ponyicsanyi, and the cover was designed by Ben Santora with art by Jeff Korleski. It was set in Optima by ExecuStaff.

Printed and bound by Haddon Craftsmen Book Manufacturing, a division of R. R. Donnelley & Sons Company.

0 9 8 7 6 5 4 3 2 1

Library of Congress Cataloging-in-Publication Data

Palda, K. Filip.
    How much is your vote worth? : the unfairness of campaign spending limits / Filip Palda.
        p.    cm.
    Includes bibliographical references.
    ISBN 1-55815-284-9 (pbk.:acid-free paper)
    1. Campaign funds—United States.    I. Title.
JK1991.P35   1994
324.7′8—dc20                                                                    93-42715
                                                                                        CIP

*For Valerie
and my loving parents*

# Contents

# Foreword

Elections are a critical part of any democratic process. How we structure the rules of our electoral system has a direct impact on the kind of life we will be able to lead. As Americans, we must ask ourselves if we are willing to take steps to provide elections that maximize our capacity to elect officials who will assist us in maintaining our nation's experiment in self-governance. Or will we be content to remain with the alternative—elections that favor the increase of "career politicians" and the growth of a bureaucratic state? This is the real issue facing us when Congress and the president consider election reform.

Today the conventional wisdom holds that money and the political action committees have corrupted and trivialized elections. As with any assumption, we must ask: Is there a hidden agenda in election reform? Will the unintended consequences of reform leave the election system worse off than before?

In his iconoclastic look at campaign finance, Filip Palda provides startling answers to these and other questions about election reform. He shows that current suggestions for reform threaten to minimize choice and further remove government from the voter. This is in addition to existing campaign finance restrictions that already handicap challengers and diminish the variety of strong candidates. The discrepancy in levels of empowerment between incumbents and challengers is central to Palda's analysis of reform methods: the setting in which campaign money is spent must be examined if we are to make rules that will provide voters with the maximum amount of information and choice. The key is not how much money is spent, but in what capacity, and by whom.

The mindset that distrusts the role of money in elections is a profoundly pessimistic one. In contrast, Palda demonstrates a deep belief in the capacity of men and women to make informed choices in order to govern their own lives. Evidence shows that Americans are not the apathetic, passive voters uninformed pundits assert. As Palda writes, "Americans are not more cynical and alienated than citizens in other countries. If anything, the reverse is true." How much is a vote worth? It should be worth enough to each of us that we will seek to maximize our opportunity for reflection and choice in every election, and to reject rules that will open the door to accident and force in the electoral process. Any kind of campaign reform rule should aim to ensure voter responsibility and participation. The vigor of representative government is essential to the security of liberty. And fair elections, which give challengers and incumbents equal advantages, are the mainstay of vigorous government.

Robert B. Hawkins, Jr., President
Institute for Contemporary Studies

# Acknowledgments

I thank Professor John G. Matsusaka of the University of Southern California and Janet Mowery, formerly of the Institute for Contemporary Studies, for their helpful comments. I thank Professor Herbert Alexander of the University of Southern California for providing me with data for Tables 2 and 3.

# 1

# *Protecting Incumbents* 在位者

> By most measures Americans pay a small cost for the
> maintenance of an adversary political process in a complicated
> federal system with its many elective offices at a variety of
> levels of government.
>
> David Adamany, *political scientist*

THIS BOOK REVIEWS FEDERAL LAWS governing election finances and asks what effect they have on political competition. The common view is that money in elections is an evil that must be tolerated but firmly controlled. To prevent the wealthy from dominating government we need contribution and spending limits, as well as public subsidies for penniless candidates. These measures are also believed to be the best way of stopping special interest groups from corrupting politicians. I argue that limits and subsidies can do just the opposite. These measures can limit what voters know about the candidates and protect incumbents from the consequences of governing badly or dishonestly.

To see how incumbents can use campaign finance laws for their own benefit we need a clear idea of what political competition is and how information affects it. The political arena is competitive when all are free to contest those in power. Candidates and independent groups of citizens contest those in power by advertising. Advertising transmits information. The amount of information which challengers or independent groups, such as Greenpeace, can get across to voters keeps incumbents alert to the needs of constituents. Spending and contribution limits interfere with this flow of information, making it harder to contest elections. This is why limits work to the advantage of those in power. In particular, limits can protect incumbents from the added criticism which advances in technology make possible. The dramatic fall in the costs of computers, telecommunications, and mass-mailing has given small groups and obscure challengers the power to move incumbents on important points of policy. A prominent example is Pat Buchanan's challenge for the 1992 Republican presidential nomination, which forced President George Bush to take a more conservative stand than he would have wished. Incumbents would rather not have to deal with such challenges.

---

"We can expect incumbents to push hard for laws that limit and control the flow of election information."

---

As a result of the threatening march of technology we can expect incumbents to push hard for laws that limit and control the flow of election information. There have been two recent attempts at reform. In 1992 Congress passed Senate Resolution 3. With great piety the bill called for subsidies, spending limits, and stricter contribution limits for members of Congress. Some Republicans attacked it as a Democratic incumbent-protection plan and President Bush vetoed it. But its main architect, Democratic senator David Boren, warned, "We'll be back." His words soon came true. On February 17, 1993, President Bill Clinton told Congress he wanted "real political reform." Two months later he announced a plan to lower certain contribution limits, give subsidies to candidates, and eliminate some loopholes in established contribution limits. This revived S3 and started a new round of reform.

Incumbents are not actively conspiring to hold on to power. Nor are they consciously rigging the rules of election finance in their favor. But many have found it easy to believe that campaign laws which "preserve stability" by keeping the same candidates and parties in power are good for the people.

Politicians warn that such stability is in danger because the people no longer respect candidates and their parties. They argue that parties reduce conflict in society and allow large numbers of people to work toward common political goals. But instead of hitting on the obvious solution, namely that parties should be more flexible and listen to what the people have to say, many politicians want to protect the parties by means of law.

Where pleas to save the parties fail, politicians—and a number of activist reformers such as those behind Common Cause—fall back on populist cries about the corrupting power of campaign money. They argue that without limits and subsidies, politics will be open only to wealthy candidates and untamed interest groups will turn elections into a confusing jungle of malicious advertising. The incumbents who make these claims conveniently forget about the government money they use every day to promote their own causes, government money granted for office staff, research, travel, and regular mailings to constituents. They also forget that jungles of any sort provide variety. The rain forest of Brazil is valued as a rich source of life-saving drugs waiting to be discovered. The political jungle gives voters a pick of many competing ideas for good government. Surely such a jungle is preferable to a desert.

The simplistic and alarmist view of election finances painted by reformers misses the crucial point that the conditions under which money is spent matter more than the amounts spent. What is important for the good of voters is that no group in society have a monopoly on expression. It is precisely such a monopoly which restrictive campaign laws can grant incumbents.

Many people who are neither reformers nor incumbents worry that government is too large and that special interests have too much influence. This is a legitimate fear, but the answer to the problem does not lie in the reform of election financing laws. The great size and growth of government invite the attention of many competing interests. Since talents and resources are not distributed evenly through society, some groups, working within the law, will find ways to profit at the expense of others. If a group can no longer influence a politician by contributing to his campaign, it will step up its efforts elsewhere, through direct lobbying or grassroots campaigns. Election finance law, no matter how enlightened, is powerless to stop such diversion of effort.

At best we can hope for a system which exposes which interest groups and politicians are on the take and who is suffering from government policies.

This book builds on these ideas. Chapter 2 reviews trends in congressional and presidential campaign spending. I suggest that the increase in spending has been taken out of context, leading to exaggeration. One needs to know not simply how fast campaign spending has been growing, but how fast it has been growing per capita, or as a fraction of GNP. Spending has also been widely confused with cost. Rising spending does not mean that costs are rising. On the contrary, there is strong evidence that election costs have fallen over the past thirty years. Cost is the effort or money it takes to get a message across to voters. Advances in communications technology have brought down the cost of disseminating information, and candidates have purchased more informational products, leading to increased spending.

Chapter 3 explains in greater detail why the transmission of information is becoming cheaper and maintains that voters are more informed about politics than before. This goes against the popular view that voters are passive recipients of easy-to-digest image advertising. It is important to recognize that there are many ways in which voters can acquire information. They can collect it individually or put their faith in an advocacy group or a magazine which specializes in drawing clear conclusions about the political choices available. The second method may leave the voter unaware of political details but in the able hands of information specialists.

Chapter 4 asks how campaign spending limits affect political competition. There is mounting evidence that challenger spending is more potent than incumbent spending. Incumbents promote themselves and build up an advantage in popular support with government resources while in office. But by election time they have exhausted the benefits that money can bring them. To protect their advantage some wish to pass a spending limit to contain the more potent challenger spending. The chapter explains not only the conflict between challengers and incumbents of the main parties, but also the conflict between the established parties and independent movements. Congress has long tried to ban or limit election spending by independent groups. I argue that spending limits may be used to entrench the established parties and protect them against outside challenges.

Chapter 5 discusses government subsidies to candidates. I argue that subsidies will not stop corruption or diminish the influence of special interest groups. Instead contributions may make candidates less responsive to the needs of their constituents, interfere with the flow of election information, and entrench the established parties at the expense of new movements.

Chapter 6 questions limits on contributions to political candidates. It is such an accepted part of conventional political wisdom that limits are needed that little thought has been given to the harm they may do. In the process of raising money candidates are forced to learn the wishes of their constituents. The traditional lament that members of Congress spend too much time raising money misses this point. The chapter also argues that the number and size of contributions a candidate receives can provide voters with vital information on how popular he or she is. Contribution limits reduce this type of information. The chapter explains the useful role of political action committees (PACs) and argues that the many complicated reporting requirements imposed by the Federal Election Commission make it hard for them to fulfil these functions.

Chapter 7 asks whether voter turnout in the United States is really too low and, if so, what should be done about it. High voter turnout in itself is not a good indicator of how healthy a democracy is. What matters is whether those who turn out are well informed about their choices. Campaign spending helps inform people, and the optimal voter turnout is that which occurs in an environment of plentiful information.

The concluding chapter summarizes the main themes of the book: that incumbents are writing election laws that will protect them against the consequences of advances in the technology of delivering information to voters, and that we must not look to election laws as a cure for electoral corruption and the excessive size of government.

# 2

# *Are Elections Too Expensive?*

No one can deny that their constituents are fed up with high-priced campaigns. These campaigns . . . involve enough spending to feed the residents of some of the smaller countries in the world for one year.

Charlie Rose, *member of Congress*

[The United States does not spend] anywhere near what other democratic countries do in their elections. We do not come near to spending what we do in this country on . . . advertising for pet food. So, in terms of priorities and importance, let us not get things out of scale. I would like to think that the value of an election for Congress or the Senate is worth as much as a can of cat food or dog food.

Robert Packwood, *senator*

HIGH CAMPAIGN COSTS ARE A favorite complaint of certain members of Congress and one that serves them well. They have used it in efforts to commandeer free advertisements from the media and to impose spending limits. They have the support of an irritated public which believes that great sums are being spent on campaigns with no productive result. Public support helps elected officials to fashion laws that work to their advantage. The tireless push by Congress to have the broadcast media sell airtime to politicians at a discount is an example of a self-serving law which, in its details, would work for incumbents and against challengers, especially challengers from minor

7

parties. This chapter explains why such cost-cutting measures benefit incumbents and work against the interest of voters.

Arguments about high election costs resemble arguments about there being too many lawyers in this country. Some who find in Japan the ingredients of economic success point out that Japan has one lawyer for every twenty in the United States. If it were harder to bring suit, they claim, the costs of doing business would fall and Americans would become more competitive. They ignore the fact that fewer companies would do business in the United States if it did not provide open legal forums in which to resolve disputes. The cost of such forums is a highly visible army of lawyers; the benefit is hidden in the smooth working of the economy. We must be open to similar possibilities in election campaigns.

Reformers have a tendency to count the costs of campaigns but ignore the benefits. Their arguments are familiar: Elections are too expensive. Candidates spend fortunes on hype and too little on the important issues. The prohibitive cost of television advertising forces politicians to compress complicated ideas and policy proposals into brief, sensational sound bites. If there were spending limits and a law restricting what broadcasters charge, candidates could afford to discuss the issues seriously and refrain from wasteful clashes of personality. Few arguments in the campaign finance debate are accepted with less scrutiny.

I argue that it is important to understand the positive functions of campaign spending. Rising campaign spending is not necessarily a cause for alarm. The observation that Congress spent 265 percent more in 1992 than it did in 1972 in real terms on campaigns is open to many interpretations. Campaign spending conveys useful information to voters and should not be confused with cost. Cost is the price of informing a given number of voters. Cost falls as advertising techniques improve. The fall in per-voter cost may lead candidates to spend *more*. Such a rise in spending may be a sign of greater competition between the candidates. To confuse expenditure with costs is to miss the point that voters can benefit from competitive campaigns where both candidates spend more as their unit costs fall. In commerce, rival firms may take advantage of better advertising techniques to launch a campaign for each other's customers. In the end, neither firm may gain much of an advantage over the other, but customers will benefit by being better informed. The political market is similar.

A review of trends in election spending in the United States, Canada, and Great Britain suggests that because of improvements in advertising technology, the price of informing voters has fallen. Even though advertisements cost more today, they reach greater numbers of people, so that the price of informing any given voter may be lower than in the past. Campaign finance regulation, however, has kept costs higher than necessary. Contribution limits have forced candidates to broaden their search for money and have prevented new candidates from using the help of large contributors to start their fledgling campaigns. Complicated reporting procedures now force candidates to spend roughly 10 percent of their campaign money filling out forms and teaching campaign workers how to comply with electoral regulation.

## Trends in Campaign Spending

Changes in campaign costs are not nearly as dramatic as the press and activist public interest groups such as Common Cause pretend.

Perhaps the first detailed study of long-term trends in election campaign costs was made by Abrams and Settle in 1978. They analyzed American presidential elections in an era before presidential spending limits (1900–1972) and found no sign that candidates as a group were spending more with each election. They found that nominal spending—spending not adjusted for the cost of living—had risen, but in real terms the 1928 and 1936 campaigns were more expensive than any until 1972. They also found that real spending per adult showed no trend whatsoever and that spending as a fraction of GNP had fallen steadily.[1]

I have done Abrams-and-Settle-style calculations for Congress for the period 1972–1992.[2] Figure 1 shows that the rise in nominal spending is more dramatic than the real rise. In fact, real spending has been constant or declining through most of the 1980s and 1990s. As Figure 2 shows, since 1978 spending per eligible voter has fluctuated without a clear pattern in the range of $2.50 to $3.50. Figure 3 confirms that the trend is similar for congressional campaign spending as a fraction of GNP. There is no

FIGURE 1
Total Spending on Congressional Campaigns, 1972–1992
(In thousands of current and 1992 dollars)

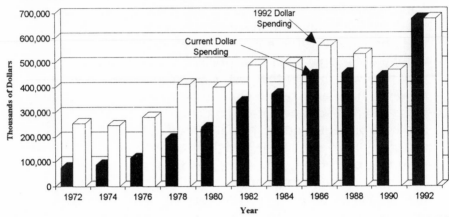

Sources: FEC press releases; U.S. Department of Commerce. *Statistical Abstract of the United States,* 1992; U.S. Department of Commerce. *Survey of Current Business,* March 1993.

FIGURE 2
Spending per Eligible Voter in Congressional Campaigns, 1972–1992
(In 1992 dollars)

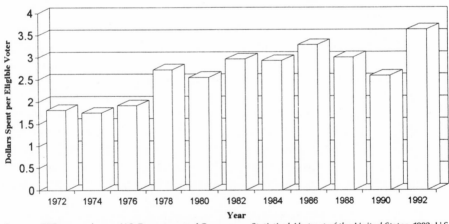

Sources: FEC press releases; U.S. Department of Commerce. *Statistical Abstract of the United States,* 1992; U.S. Department of Commerce. *Survey of Current Business,* March 1993.

doubt that campaign spending has risen since the early 1970s, but alarmists have exaggerated the rise. As a population and an economy grow, it is natural that spending grows too. Unless this is kept in mind it is easy to claim that spending is rising too quickly and that this rise shows that politicians are selling out

FIGURE 3
Congressional Campaign Spending as a Fraction of GNP, 1972–1992

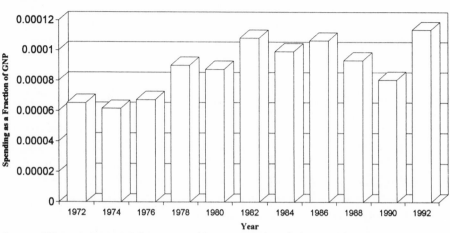

*Sources:* FEC press releases; U.S. Department of Commerce. *Statistical Abstract of the United States,* 1992; U.S. Department of Commerce. *Survey of Current Business,* March 1993.

ever more to special interests. Such alarmist portrayals lead naturally to calls for campaign cost-cutting proposals.

## History of Cost-cutting Proposals

The earliest proposals to regulate election costs appeared at the dawn of political radio advertising. Calvin Coolidge made the first radio political broadcast in 1926 (Rothschild 1978). Twelve years later Frank Knox declared that both major parties should get free airtime. Knox was Republican Alf Landon's running mate in 1936. His campaign experience convinced him that forcing radio stations to give away airtime was the best way to keep costs down.

The movement to ration and evenly distribute airtime picked up speed after Eisenhower demonstrated what a well-organized TV ad campaign could accomplish. Democratic members of Congress have been the main proponents of free airtime, probably because Republicans are better fundraisers. Democrats revised political programming laws in 1972 to make sure that candidates did not have to pay more than commercial advertisers. Over the years members of Congress have tried to introduce stronger laws that would give candidates discounted or free airtime. In 1991, five Senate resolutions (S3, S6, S7, S128, and S143) were proposed to control the price of TV ads. Most of these resolutions were the work of Democrats, but Senate Resolution 7, which called for free airtime, was the creation of Republican senator Bob Dole.

What distinguishes Democratic and Republican proposals for free time is the larger package of laws of which they form a part. In addition to free time, Democrats want campaign spending limits, limits on TV advertising, and subsidies. Republicans only want cheap or free airtime. Cheaper airtime without spending limits would amplify the power of Republican wealth, because Republicans could buy relatively more of the inexpensive airtime. Spending limits would undo the Republican advantage and allow Democrats to run safer, less expensive contests. David L. Boren, one of the chief Democratic sponsors of S3, explained that Democrats insist on linking broadcast discounts and spending limits because "if you cut the rate in half, they'll just spend twice as much unless you cap overall spending" (Alston 1991, p. 137).

In spite of these efforts Congress has not managed to pass a law that forces broadcast discounts. But Congress does manage to intimidate broadcasters. After the 1990 elections a Federal Communications Commission audit of thirty radio and TV stations in five big-city markets found that candidates paid more for comparable advertising time than commercial clients at sixteen of twenty television stations.[3] Congress used the report to threaten legislation. The threat was enough to send TV rates down by as much as 30 percent in many markets (Alston 1991, p. 137). Broadcasters feared that without this costly gesture they may have faced even more unpleasant laws.

### Media Rates

The reaction to the FCC audit shows how ready members of Congress are to believe that the media are uncompetitive. This belief serves them well and is not shaken by the fact of thousands of radio and TV stations competing for advertising dollars. An outraged Democratic media consultant claimed, "Television stations have abused political advertisers for years" (Alston 1991, p. 138). Such inaccurate statements are common.

What should we make of the audit by the Federal Communications Commission that showed TV stations charging candidates more for the same time slots than they charge private companies? The audit embarrassed many broadcasters and gave Congress new energy in its drive to lower costs. But this does not show that stations exploit candidates desperate for election and that only the law can restrain broadcasters.

The law was written when stations sold advertising time according to a schedule of common rates. In those days it was easy to specify what "comparable advertising time" meant. Today, pricing is more complicated and reflects the greater number of options which advertisers offer. Stations do not set rates but offer slots by auction to bidders. A client will bid low for the 8:00 P.M. prime-time slot if he or she is prepared to be bumped without notice. Such "immediately preemptible time" is cheap but unreliable. Candidates prefer to buy fixed time, late in the campaign season, because they want to be sure they can answer unexpected attacks. They pay a premium for this privilege.

The FCC found that one station charged candidates $4,000 for the same spots commercial clients won with bids of $570 to $2,550 (Alston 1991, p. 139). These differences look shocking if one is not aware of the basis on which candidates bought their time. Had the FCC audit been refined to distinguish between fixed and preemptible time categories, it might have found no evidence that candidates were being charged more than other advertisers.

Alston gives another example of the complex rate system which may make it too difficult for the FCC to monitor comparable media time. "A station controls four thirty-second spots on a show. A campaign and two regular commercial clients each pay $800 for a spot, but the station has to dump the fourth slot for $500 just to fill it. The candidate is now entitled to a $300 rebate because $500 has become the lowest unit rate for that show" (Alston 1991, p. 139). Problems like these may convince Congress to pursue its simpler, larger goal of free time, rather than "fair" time.

### The Self-interest behind Cost Reforms

Legislators usually bundle free airtime in complicated campaign law packages. They recognize that the same rule can work to the advantage of different parties depending on the details of the package. Without spending limits, artificially cheap time gives an advantage to politicians with money. This is why Democrats want spending limits to accompany free-airtime rules. Republicans raise more money and would have more to gain from a cheap airtime rule without spending limits.

Although the two main parties bicker over the details, they close ranks against independent challenges. The Senate Elections Ethics Act, or S3, a package of laws which Congress passed but the president vetoed in 1992, would have given "eligible" Senate candidates the right to buy broadcast time at half the normal rate.[4] President Clinton's 1993 reform proposal was similar. Eligible candidates are almost exclusively candidates from the two major parties. Independents would have had trouble meeting conditions such as the provision that they had to spend $250,000 to be considered for a variety of subsidies.

Congress could not bind independents with spending limits for fear of violating the First Amendment's guarantee of free speech. Independents had to remain free to buy as much time as they wished. This right would have lost value in the face of the benefits S3 proposed for eligible (i.e., major party) candidates. Eligible Senate candidates who bound themselves to limits would have received handsome government campaign subsidies from a "Make Democracy Work Fund." They would also have qualified for airtime sold at half rate. The package would have affected political competition on two levels. It would have protected Democrats against Republicans, and it would have protected insiders against challenges from independent candidates—as well as relieving incumbents of the work of raising funds.

Laws such as S3 which discriminate against outsiders are firmly in the tradition of American broadcast regulation. The FCC's now defunct Fairness Doctrine forced broadcasters to provide their audiences with "reasonable opportunity for the presentation of opposing [political] viewpoints."[5] According to Ranney, "Broadcasters found it easiest to comply with this rule by treating every issue as having two sides, no more and no less, and by following coverage of one side's case with coverage of the other side's" (1990, p. 196). The two sides were invariably Democratic and Republican.

Established parties in other countries have passed less subtle laws, reflecting more clearly their self-interested inclinations. Canadian parliamentary contests divide 6.5 hours of free airtime among the parties in proportion to how well each party did in the previous election. The same principle rations the amount of airtime parties may buy. The minor parties, especially the Reform party, which grew dramatically after the 1988 election, complain that the law builds in advantages based on outdated past performance in elections.

For members of the two main parties, the issue is how to tilt the playing field in their own favor. Democrats battle Republicans over details that could work to one party's advantage. The only thing both parties agree on is that outsiders and independents should be discriminated against. In this pursuit they have the support of prominent academics. Larry Sabato, one of the intellectual defenders of election finance regulation, is proud to claim that "two-party advocates, such as this author, who believe that the two-party system serves as a bulwark against fragmentation that often paralyses countries as diverse as the United States, see nothing wrong in discriminating against third parties when it comes to free media and public financing" (1989, p. 36). This type of argument and the public's undisputed notion that campaign costs are too high help members of Congress in their battle to legislate free media time.

## Costs Are Not Expenses

It is easy to confuse the cost of campaigning with the final amount spent on a campaign. A seasoned political reporter writes without hesitation that "the cost of running for federal office skyrocketed in the 1980s primarily because of the high price of television advertising, direct-mail operations, special public opinion polling, and campaign consultants. All of which are seen as necessary components of a successful campaign" (*Elections '88,* 1989b, p. 122). This is incorrect and leads to the false impression that campaigns are wasteful and becoming even more so.

Cost is the monetary and material expense of achieving a certain result. In the case of an election, the result in question is communication with the public. A yardstick, or unit, of communication, such as how well voters remember a candidate after five days, or how many thousands of households are reached, allows one to speak of the per-unit cost of campaigning: how many dollars the candidate must spend to reach a given number of people. Costs are *given* to the candidate, and he can do nothing to affect them. They are distinct from spending, which is simply the dollar outlay a candidate *chooses* for his campaign.

This way of looking at costs makes it difficult to accept the urgent need for so-called cost-cutting measures such as broadcast discounts, subsidies, or spending limits. Under the Senate Elections Ethics Act, proposed in 1990 by the Democrats, broadcasters would sell airtime at half price to eligible Senate candidates. The act rested on the premise that lower costs lead to lower spending. It is just as likely that when costs fall spending will rise. As Peter Fenn, a Democratic media consultant, explains, "If people think they are going to reduce the cost of campaigns by reducing the price of a TV spot, they are sadly mistaken. That is the great fallacy. The answer is, you'll buy more time" (Alston 1991, p. 137). After the 1990 FCC audit, rates fell, and this generated savings for candidates. Most political clients of the TV stations "spent the money to buy huge [TV] schedules" (Alston 1991, p. 137).

If all candidates are equally matched, an increase in the costs of informing voters may not necessarily lead to more spending. The situation can be compared to a tennis match during which the sun emerges from the clouds to distract both players. If both players are equally affected nothing has really changed and there is no reason to choose a different level of effort. If, however, one of the players performs better in the sun, he may choose to exert himself more and his opponent may choose a lower level of effort. The overall level of effort (or campaign spending in the case of an election) depends on unit costs and on how much the candidates wish to spend.[6]

### The Bright Side of Costs

Fundraising has a bad name, but it may be one of the best things a candidate can do for his constituents. This may seem odd at first, and it is perhaps more natural to believe, as Hedrick Smith does, that "except for the exceptionally wealthy, raising political money has become a throbbing headache that drains the vital time and energy from the job of governing. This chore leaves many members part-time legislators and full-time fundraisers" (1988, p. 154). Smith's comment shows how hard it is to shake the old-fashioned notion that politicians are most productive when sitting in the legislature. But governing wisely is not just a matter of drafting laws. Politicians must know what their constituents want. Raising funds is one of the best ways of finding this out.

There are incentives built into the political market that force candidates to inform themselves. If a candidate strays too far from public desires he will lose contributions to competing candidates and advocacy groups. The popularity of sophisticated marketing techniques developed for mass-mail fundraising campaigns shows how intensely candidates feel the need to know their market. Candidates do not enjoy fundraising any more than children enjoy their homework, but this does not mean that the time they spend is wasted. It is perhaps not surprising that to spare themselves the effort of raising these funds candidates should favor free airtime rules. Such rules may allow candidates to play hooky on their constituents.

It is not only candidates who learn from the process. The money they raise allows them to inform voters through advertising. Candidates place a high value on advertising because they find it an effective way of getting information to voters. Advertising is of value to voters because it lowers their costs of collecting information about the issues and the candidates, making it easier for them to choose intelligently (Husted, Kenny, and Morton 1991, 1992, Matsusaka and Palda 1992b, and Rothschild 1978).

Recent advances in communications technology illustrate how productive it can be to spend time on fundraising and money on advertising. Cheap, powerful computers and campaign software now allow candidates without much money to run efficient campaigns of the sort which only well-backed incumbents could afford in the 1970s. Computer systems allow campaign workers to maintain lists of supporters and contributors in keeping with the special needs of the campaign (*Elections '88,* 1989a, p. 135). Candidates can run "interactive" campaigns in which their volunteers identify the issues that worry voters and feed the information to a computer. The computer draws on the candidate's platform to tailor letters addressing the concerns of each individual. As one prominent political consultant said of the new technology, "One of the effects of professionals in campaigns is to increase the amount of information people have about candidates, particularly at the local level. Twenty years ago candidates spent their money on junk—mass letters, yard signs, and bumper stickers. That had nothing to do with the issues. . . . Today [using computers], I can actually get each person a specific message about the issue he or she cares about" (*Elections '88*, 1989, p. 138). The advance of technology has also freed campaign workers from record keeping and other drudgery. "When half your resources aren't being spent doing menial data management, volunteers are freed to do more people-to-people work. So you have better grass-roots politics," said a GOP computer specialist (*Elections '88*, 1989, p. 138).

---

"Advertising is of value to voters because it lowers their costs of collecting information about the issues and the candidates, making it easier for them to choose intelligently."

---

These advances in technology suggest that campaign costs have actually *fallen* per unit of information. This is not surprising. Technological advances allow tasks to be performed more efficiently—that is, at a lower cost. In politics these advances help candidates to reach a given number of people with less expense than before. The benefit of lower costs is that now voters are better informed *for every dollar* a candidate spends. *How many dollars* that candidate chooses to spend is a separate issue and must not be blamed on rising costs. It should instead be attributed to the increasing benefit of campaign spending, both for the candidate and for the voter.

### Wars of Attrition

This rosy picture is open to one major criticism. Some researchers believe that what matters to election outcomes is *relative* spending (Carter and Racine 1990). If one candidate doubles campaign spending his or her chances of winning go up, but if both candidates spend more their chances do not diverge very far. Under these conditions two very different types of campaigns can lead to the same outcome. If there are two similar candidates and neither candidate spends anything, voters will be at a loss as to which one is the better choice. They will flip a coin or abstain. The chances of victory are even. If each spends $1 million, voters will have a pretty good picture of both candidates and will recognize that they are similar. Voters will be indifferent and will flip a coin or abstain. In the first case voters have no information; in the second case they have almost complete information. But information does not affect the chances of either candidate's victory. Would it not be better to save society the expense of a pitched election battle and limit what candidates spend?

This argument is well known to students of arms races. Enemies at first face each other with clubs and stones. Technology advances and both sides invest in new and usually more expensive arms to maintain a balance of power. With or without weapons both sides are equally safe, but the society relying on heavy modern arms pays more for its safety.

The analogy with campaigns is misleading because weapons do not lead to the manufacture of beneficial products. Campaign spending and advances in advertising produce, among other things, leaders of high quality. An extreme example posits a situation in which there are no media. Candidates can only spend money traveling from doorstep to doorstep. Few people in a congressional district will know who is running. The views and characters of the candidates cannot influence the election, because it is too hard for voters to learn what they are. Criminals and saints have the same chance of winning office. If there are more criminals than saints in this world, the chances are that criminals will dominate Congress. If all of a sudden, however, television is invented, criminals will lose. Parties will look for saints to run as their candidates.

Advances in the technology of delivering information allow voters to choose more accurately the candidates who fulfill their ideals. Bad candidates are eliminated and good ones appointed, with all the good candidates having much in common. Perhaps American politicians and parties seem similar because of a long spell of Darwinian selection driven by increasingly sophisticated media.

## Laws That Increase Costs

Perhaps the only force working against falling costs is campaign law. It is no secret to regulators or even to the most interventionist politician that economic regulations make it expensive to do business. Politics is like business in many ways and cannot avoid the burdens that come with regulation. This leap in reasoning from economics to politics is hard for some. Several recent books by experts in campaign finance do not even mention that complicated, restrictive regulatory laws may raise costs.[7]

A report by Harvard's Campaign Finance Study Group emphasized that "The Federal Election Campaign Act has itself increased the costs of election campaigning in two ways. Costs of compliance with the Act divert scarce resources from activities which involve communications with voters. And, more significantly, in strictly limiting the amounts of money that individuals can contribute to campaigns, the Act has unintentionally increased the costs of raising campaign funds" (Campaign Finance Study Group 1979, pp. 1–17).

There are two sorts of compliance cost. The most visible is the cost of reporting campaign contributions. Candidates must report their loans, contributions, gifts in kind, and expenditures to the Federal Election Commission (FEC). Any contribution of more than $200 by an individual must be reported to the FEC along with the donor's name, address, employer, occupation, and place of business. Contributions from PACs must be reported in greater detail. Figure 4 shows examples of the types of forms and some of the bewildering details about their benefactors that candidates must supply to the FEC. It is not enough simply to say how much money was received. Money comes in many forms: cash, gifts in kind, loans. Loans from individuals are considered contributions until repaid, but those from banks are, under certain circumstances, not considered contributions. These and many other details must be carefully itemized. Similar detail is required in reporting a candidate's expenditure.

FIGURE 4
## Report of Receipts and Disbursements for an Authorized Commitee

| SCHEDULE A — ITEMIZED RECEIPTS Contributions from Individuals/Persons | Use separate schedule(s) for each category of the Detailed Summary Page | PAGE 3 OF 3 FOR LINE NUMBER 11(a)(i) |
|---|---|---|

Any information copied from such Reports and Statements may not be sold or used by any person for the purpose of soliciting contributions or for commercial purposes, other than using the name and address of any political committee to solicit contributions from such committee.

NAME OF COMMITTEE (in Full)
Sam Jones for Congress    C00015551

| Full Name, Mailing Address and ZIP Code | Name of Employer / Occupation / Aggregate Year-to-Date | Date (month, day, year) | Amount of Each Receipt this Period |
|---|---|---|---|
| **A.** Dominic Romano 267 Monastery Close City, State  ZIP CODE Receipt For: [X] Primary [ ] General [ ] Other (specify): | St. Dismas College / theologian / Aggregate Year-to-Date > $ 2,000.00 | 6-8-88 7-25-88 | $2,000 MEMO ($1,000)MEMO |
| **B.** Dominic Romano--REDESIGNATION OF ABOVE Receipt For: [ ] Primary [X] General [ ] Other (specify): | / / Aggregate Year-to-Date > $ 2,000.00 | 7-25-88 | $1,000 MEMO |
| **C.** Geoffrey Peebles--REATTRIBUTION 18 Lancaster Terrace City, State  ZIP CODE Receipt For: [X] Primary [ ] General [ ] Other (specify): | Gold, White & Green / interior designer / Aggregate Year-to-Date > $ 750.00 | 6-24-88 8-3-88 | $1,500 MEMO ($ 750)MEMO |
| **D.** Margo Peebles--REATTRIBUTION address same as above Receipt For: [X] Primary [ ] General [ ] Other (specify): | Weekly Flash / reporter / Aggregate Year-to-Date > $ 750.00 | 8-3-88 | $750 MEMO |
| **E.** Receipt For: [ ] Primary [ ] General [ ] Other (specify): | / / Aggregate Year-to-Date > $ | | |
| **F.** Receipt For: [ ] Primary [ ] General [ ] Other (specify): | / / Aggregate Year-to-Date > $ | | |
| **G.** Receipt For: [ ] Primary [ ] General [ ] Other (specify): | / / Aggregate Year-to-Date > $ | | |

SUBTOTAL of Receipts This Page (optional) ..........................................   ----0----

TOTAL This Period (last page this line number only) ..................................   $3,292.89

continued on next page

FIGURE 4 (continued)

| SCHEDULE B          ITEMIZED DISBURSEMENTS | | Use separate schedule(s) for each category of the Detailed Summary Page | PAGE 1    OF 1 |
|---|---|---|---|
| Operating Expenditures | | | FOR LINE NUMBER 17 |

Any information copied from such Reports and Statements may not be sold or used by any person for the purpose of soliciting contributions or for commercial purposes, other than using the name and address of any political committee to solicit contributions from such committee.

**NAME OF COMMITTEE (in Full)**

Sam Jones for Congress   C00015551

| A. Full Name, Mailing Address and ZIP Code | Purpose of Disbursement | Date (month, day, year) | Amount of Each Disbursement This Period |
|---|---|---|---|
| Arcadia Savings and Loan 2550 Fiduciary Square City, State   ZIP CODE | interest on loan  Disbursement for: ☐ Primary ☐ General ☐ Other (specify) | 7-5-88 8-12-88 | $84.95 $81.09 |
| **B. Full Name, Mailing Address and ZIP Code** | Purpose of Disbursement | Date (month, day, year) | Amount of Each Disbursement This Period |
| Concepts Inc. 345 Vista Street City, State   ZIP CODE | campaign literature  Disbursement for: ☐ Primary ☐ General ☐ Other (specify) | 7-6-88 | $562.79 |
| **C. Full Name, Mailing Address and ZIP Code** | Purpose of Disbursement | Date (month, day, year) | Amount of Each Disbursement This Period |
| U.S. Postmaster Pinehill Post Office City, State   ZIP CODE | postage  Disbursement for: ☐ Primary ☐ General ☐ Other (specify) | 7-8-88 8-20-88 | $45.91 $54.09 |
| **D. Full Name, Mailing Address and ZIP Code** | Purpose of Disbursement | Date (month, day, year) | Amount of Each Disbursement This Period |
| Norbert Jones (contributor) 1738 Pinehill Crescent City, State   ZIP CODE | dinner for staff  Disbursement for: ☐ Primary ☐ General ☐ Other (specify) | 7-18-88 | $57.89 in-kind received |
| **E. Full Name, Mailing Address and ZIP Code** | Purpose of Disbursement | Date (month, day, year) | Amount of Each Disbursement This Period |
| Pinehill Realty Co. 444 Washington Street City, State   ZIP CODE | rent for campaign HQ  Disbursement for: ☐ Primary ☐ General ☐ Other (specify) | 7-20-88 8-22-88 | $800.00 $800.00 |
| **F. Full Name, Mailing Address and ZIP Code** | Purpose of Disbursement | Date (month, day, year) | Amount of Each Disbursement This Period |
| ZAPCOM 77700 Graham Highway City, State   ZIP CODE | telephone services  Disbursement for: ☐ Primary ☐ General ☐ Other (specify) | 7-26-88 | $653.56 |
| **G. Full Name, Mailing Address and ZIP Code** | Purpose of Disbursement | Date (month, day, year) | Amount of Each Disbursement This Period |
| Sam Jones (contributor) 6288 Pinehill Street City, State   ZIP CODE | campaign pens  Disbursement for: ☐ Primary ☐ General ☐ Other (specify) | 8-17-88 | $279.83 in-kind received |
| **H. Full Name, Mailing Address and ZIP Code** | Purpose of Disbursement | Date (month, day, year) | Amount of Each Disbursement This Period |
| MasterCard Second State Bank Three Municipal Plaza City, State   ZIP CODE | see below  Disbursement for: ☐ Primary ☐ General ☐ Other (specify) | 8-18-88 | $1,742.64 |
| **I. Full Name, Mailing Address and ZIP Code** | Purpose of Disbursement | Date (month, day, year) | Amount of Each Disbursement This Period |
| Dryden's Restaurant 875 Pope Street City, State   ZIP CODE | fundraising dinner  Disbursement for: ☐ Primary ☐ General ☐ Other (specify) | 7-2-88 | $1,742.64 MEMO |

SUBTOTAL of Disbursements This Page (optional) ......................................................

TOTAL This Period (last page this line number only) .................................................. | $5,162.75

Source: FEC, *Campaign Guide for Congressional Candidates and Committees*, July 1988.

Congressional candidates must make quarterly reports in election years and biannual reports in other years. In election years presidential candidates must report every month. Any contribution of $1,000 or more made at least twenty days into the congressional candidate's campaign must be reported within forty-eight hours in writing to the Clerk of the House of Representatives or the Secretary of the Senate. In addition to filling out forms, campaign workers must educate themselves to make sure they are obeying the law. The cost not only of complying, but of ensuring *correct* compliance, is a significant part of all campaigns. In the mid-1980s presidential campaigns devoted roughly 10 percent of their budgets to compliance (Alexander and Haggerty 1987, p. 188).

Candidates are not the only ones to be encumbered. PACs must go through a similar procedure, reporting from whom they get money and to whom they give it. PACs must itemize each independent expenditure of more than $200. An independent expenditure is an expenditure for a communication which expressly advocates the election or defeat of a candidate. Any other group or individual not belonging to a PAC must in each reporting period (four times in election years) provide notarized reports of independent spending exceeding $250 and certify in writing that this expenditure is truly independent. Any independent expenditures of more than $1,000 made twenty days into the campaign must be reported to Congress within twenty-four hours. The catalogue of reporting rules continues through sixty-two clearly written but highly detailed pages of the FEC *Campaign Guide for Congressional Candidates and Committees.*[8]

---

"Candidates spend so much of their time fund-raising not because advertising rates are high but because contributions of more than $1,000 from nonparty PACs and individuals are forbidden."

---

### Congress

All of this reporting is to ensure that candidates stick to their contribution limits. Obeying these limits imposes a further burden. Candidates spend so much of their time fundraising not because advertising rates are high but because contributions of more than $1,000 from nonparty PACs and individuals are forbidden. As former Republican representative Dick Cheney wrote of the presidential race, "It simply takes a great deal more effort to raise $10–15 million, if it only comes in amounts of $1,000 or less, than it does if there are no upper limits on the amount an individual can contribute. Time spent on fundraising activities . . . detracts from the basic purpose of the campaign—persuading a majority of the voters to support a particular candidate" (Cheney 1980, p. 244). Of his own problems as a congressional candidate Cheney wrote, "The $1,000 limit makes it very difficult for a newcomer to raise sufficient funds to get his campaign off the ground. The result is that a would-be candidate finds it necessary to finance his beginning efforts himself because no one else will, especially if he is running against an incumbent or in a primary" (Cheney, p. 245). These problems are particularly grave for outsiders such as independent candidates, which may throw light on why to date so few of this breed have been seen in modern American politics.

### The Presidency

Presidential candidates are squeezed on both sides. They can accept only so much, and if they take public subsidies, they can spend only so much. Obeying spending limits in primaries and conventions is particularly complicated. There is a different limit on what can be spent in any state. These limits for states bear almost no relation to how important those states are for the candidates or the value of the information voters may derive from races in those states. New Hampshire is the most closely watched of all primaries, but candidates who get public funds are limited to spending no more than sixteen cents per voter there. So candidates advertise from Massachussetts, where they pay more than they would have to if they could spend freely in New Hampshire. A further complication is that the candidate cannot spend up to the limit in each state. He faces an overall spending limit which is roughly half the sum of individual state limits.

### Independent Groups

Limits also hinder independent groups. Independent PACs cannot accept sums of more than $5,000 and cannot give more than $1,000 to any candidate. Movements are less effective if they cannot pool their members' resources and direct them in concentrated bursts. The law has forced them to set up and administer multiple committees, and it is estimated that it may cost 10 percent more to raise and spend the same amount of money as it did before the Federal Election Campaign Act (Moore 1980, p. 58). In order to publicize their viewpoint, many of these groups now have to buy their own advertising during elections. This may be a less effective way of getting information across about their preferred candidate than simply giving the money to the candidate to spend. The loss in efficiency is hard to measure but may reduce the flow of relevant election information.

## Unintended Consequences

In sum, election rules and reporting requirements have raised the cost of searching for money, of giving it, and of spending it. These constraints have made it more expensive to get information across to voters. The principle at work is that a regulation restricting the use of efficient methods for getting a job done makes the job harder to do.

The law has also had unexpected consequences for the way campaigns are run and where power is concentrated. Limits were meant to keep large contributors from "buying" candidates. Instead they have made it hard for challengers to contest incumbents. A large part of the cost of compliance goes to overhead, such as renting office space, buying furniture and computers, and assembling a competent team of experts to do the paperwork. The overhead is an obstacle to *all* candidates, but it is harder for new, poor candidates because they cannot spread the fixed expense of administration over a high volume of paperwork. As detailed in Chapter 6, there is little evidence that campaign contributions "buy" candidates. Greater danger lies in costly election rules which make it hard for challengers to contest incumbents. They have also led to the growth of large, highly centralized campaign headquarters and the decline of interest in organizing grassroots support.

The amount spent on a campaign is not a figure which in itself should give alarm. The arguments incumbents use to justify cost-cutting measures such as broadcast discounts and spending limits overlook the fact that campaign spending brings information to voters. The next chapter explains in more detail the role of political information.

# 3

# *How Money Gets the Word Out*

Cherish . . . the spirit of your people and keep alive their
attention. . . . If once they become inattentive to public
affairs, you and I, and Congress and Assemblies, Judges and
Governors, shall all become wolves.

Thomas Jefferson

ELECTION LAW IN THE UNITED States today puts few direct restraints
on a candidate's freedom of speech. There are no official mandatory
spending limits, and the limits on political contributions are weak.
This is not what legislators intended two decades ago. In 1974
Congress amended the Federal Election Campaign Act. The revised
act imposed spending and contributions limits, expanded
campaign subsidies to presidential candidates, and outlawed
independent political spending by private citizens who advocated
the election or defeat of a candidate or party. The act was an
elaborate effort by incumbents to control the flow of information
in elections. In 1976 the Supreme Court ruled large parts of the
act unconstitutional on the grounds that "a restriction on the
amount of money a person or a group can spend on political communication during a campaign necessarily reduces the quantity
of expression by restricting the number of issues discussed, the
depth of their exploration and the size of the audience reached.
This is because virtually every means of communicating ideas in
today's mass society requires expenditure of money" (*Buckley v.
Valeo,* pp. 634–35).

Most members of Congress were not grateful for the Supreme Court's insight and have worked hard ever since to bring back and amplify the 1974 law. Their efforts have shown little sense of how people collect information or why candidates choose to transmit it. This is distressing because the stakes riding on political outcomes grow with the size of government. And as the stakes rise, so does the value of information. The main idea behind election law should be that campaigns must allow candidates and constituents to learn about each other.

---

"Contributions themselves are a form of opinion poll, and subsidies interfere with the quality of information by reducing candidates' incentives to test their popularity by raising money."

---

Campaigns send valuable signals to voters. Competitive elections give politicians a strong incentive to provide information at low cost to voters, while voters have methods of evaluating political signals. These signals help large numbers of citizens to coordinate their actions at little cost. When voters use election information to act in concert they can impose discipline on their representatives. This is why policy makers with the public's interest at heart must be alert to the effect that campaign regulation will have on the flow of information.

Spending limits are obvious threats to knowledge, but other laws such as contributions limits and campaign subsidies can also do damage. This is seldom recognized because of a tendency to believe that information is transmitted mainly through radio and television advertisements—the main activities affected by spending limits. But information is transmitted through other channels as well. Polls are a valuable way of finding out what people think about the candidates and of deriving information from those opinions. Contributions themselves are a form of opinion poll, and subsidies interfere with the quality of information by reducing candidates' incentives to test their popularity by raising money. Regulating contributions and subsidizing candidates can thus work against the welfare of voters.

Another firmly entrenched belief which leads reformers to discount the value of campaign information is that current methods of communicating with voters stimulate more emotion than thought. Image advertising and the shrinking of complicated policies into slogans seem to violate the traditional ideal: candidates who spell out their platforms for voters. In this chapter I present evidence which suggests that the way candidates promote themselves is an intelligent response to the problem of communicating with people who do not have time to explore policy details. I also suggest that voters are not poorly informed and that they can get valuable knowledge from independent sources such as newpapers, opinion polls, and other voters.

## The Myth of the Uninformed Voter

What voters know about their candidates determines how government spends its budget and writes regulations. As government grows, so does the voters' stake in choosing a representative. Any party that wishes to control a public purse worth a third of GNP can expect questions about what it intends to do. Voters and the press ask these questions because the high stakes make information valuable.

The steady growth of government over the past fifty years has increased the import of elections to the point that we might expect the American electorate to have become more informed about politics. But by popular accounts the reverse has happened. Americans are said to be less interested in and informed about politics than in the past. This leaves them vulnerable to campaign propaganda and tilts the playing field in favor of those who have the money to impose their agenda. Some critics blame voter ignorance on mindless, sensational political advertising which focuses on images and ignores issues. The candidate's ideas and platform are presented only in a haze, but through these superficial advertisements candidates can increase voter demand for their services. It is important not to be outspent because, as students of campaign advertising put it, "persuasive communications" can change attitudes.

John Kenneth Galbraith's argument that firms can brain-wash consumers with advertising to create demand for useless products has a strong grip on critics of campaign management. Their predictable solution is to bring an end to thirty-second broadcast advertising attacks, impose spending limits so that candidates are forced to make wiser use of their money, and subsidize campaigns to relieve candidates of the pressure to raise money through sensationalism.[1]

These proposals thrive even though there is no firm support for the notion that voters are uninformed, that images carry less information than a presentation of issues, and that politicians try to mold voter preferences. A growing body of statistical research rejects these notions and provides grounds for rejecting government control of political information.

### Rational Ignorance

Voters probably find it useful to be selectively ignorant. Other-wise image advertising would play a small part in the education of the voter. Voters need images to choose a candidate of ability and integrity. A candidate with these qualities does not always need to be supervised or questioned. This eases the voter's burden of exploring what a favored candidate thinks on every issue. As Donald Wittman observes, "A voter needs to know little about the actions of his congressman in order to make intelligent choices in the election. It is sufficient for the voter to find a person or organization(s) with similar preferences and then ask advice on how to vote. For example, people who like to hunt are more likely to read the literature from the National Rifle Association than from an organization attempting to ban guns" (1989).

Finding an able candidate is important because no one knows what all the issues are or what they will be in the future. It is too costly for candidates to spell out every possible choice they will make while in office, and it is too expensive for voters to form an opinion about every contingency. The search for the candidate who will make, on average, the right choices as situations develop is the search for an able candidate.

Ultimately voters should care only about the issues. But they cannot afford to believe a candidate without evidence about his character. Testimonials from important people and scenes of large, enthusiastic followings are a candidate's credentials.

Without good credentials the candidate cannot make credible promises. As a result, many political ads are a mix of image (credentials) and issue.

Those who lament the increase in voter ignorance blame image advertising. But content analysis of elections suggests that issues are not as neglected as many believe.[2] Joslyn found that issues surfaced in 77 percent of the television political ads he analyzed (1980). Patterson and McLure found issues referred to in 70 percent of television advertisements in the 1972 presidential campaign (1976). In an original study, Faber and Storey discovered that in the 1984 Texas contest for governor, voters were more likely to remember issues than images (1984).

Bennet has noted that talking about the issues is not the same as taking a stand on them (1977). This refers to the traditional view, supported by some research, that by sending vague messages candidates may avoid alienating certain voters, while at the same time projecting an image of seriousness and sincerity. There is growing evidence, however, that taking a stand on issues may be a better campaign strategy than being vague. Patton and Smith compared candidates who did not take stands with those who did and found that those who took no stand were not highly rated by voters (1980). Rosen and Einhorn found that voters considered candidates who did not take a stand to be less honest, less direct, and less well informed than their opponents who did take a stand (1972). In experiments with volunteers, Rudd found that voters give higher ratings to candidates with more precise positions on the issues (1989). Mansfield and Hale found that voters form their opinions about candidates by combining what they know about the image of the candidates with what they know about those candidates' positions on the issues (1986). Voters are interested in where their politicians stand, but positions cannot be separated from questions of integrity and ability, that is, the candidate's image.

Jean Crete (1991) summarized a broad range of research in the following propositions:

1. Election advertising increases voters' knowledge of issues and candidates.
2. Message repetition (frequency) is an important factor in familiarizing voters with candidates and issues.

3.  There is a connection between the issues candidates propose in their advertising and the issues the electorate cares about.
4.  Candidates who take a position on the issues in their advertising rate higher with the electorate than candidates who do not.

## The Optimal Amount of Ignorance

Voters cannot be perfectly informed on all the issues. This means we must expect them to be ignorant about some issues. What is the right, or optimal, amount of ignorance? This depends on the costs and benefits to each voter of electing the right candidate. A voter must first decide how much effort to invest in making the right political choice and then must choose a method for making that choice. When there is a great deal at stake, as there might be in a state referendum on abortion, the voter may decide to set aside considerable time and exert substantial effort to inform himself. He must choose among many potentially suitable methods of gathering the information he will need. The method he chooses depends on the type of person he is. Education, interest in political details and drama, and distraction by family matters may all have a bearing on how one answers the crucial questions "Do I invest heavily in finding a candidate or advocacy group I can trust to think for me, or do I inform myself independently, in detail, on every issue?"

It is tempting to conclude that someone who knows little about the technical details behind issues is uninformed. In fact, the method people choose to make up their minds at the ballot box reveals only how informed they *appear* to be. But the quality of their choices is difficult to gauge from such appearances. It is important to look at the personal traits that influence the way in which a voter gathers information.

**Ease and pleasure in evaluating issues.**    The more educated a voter is, the more facility and pleasure he may experience in following political details. Such a voter has less need to delegate the responsibility for thinking to the candidate. Faber and Storey found that educated voters remembered more about what challengers had to say than uneducated voters did. Educated voters want to hear opposing views and are not satisfied with what their elected officials tell them. Faber and Storey also found that education increased recall of issue advertising but not of image advertising. The message is that education attunes one to issues.

Less-educated voters may be unable or unwilling to get their information in the same way, but this does not mean that the quality of their political choices will be lower. Their best recourse may be to invest heavily in deciding whom to trust. Images may be very important in this regard. Signs of integrity and confidence in the candidate are important cues to such voters. The opinions of trusted sources such as friends, the local newspaper, or established public interest groups will also be important guides.

**The value of time.**     Someone with a high salary and a career showing great potential may have little time for anything but work. Such a person may prefer to find a candidate to trust or a specialized, partisan source of news, such as the newsletter of a public policy think tank, to guide him. His knowledge of ongoing issues may be superficial, but he will have invested strongly in learning who to listen to. As a result the quality of his political choices may be high.

**Competing interests.**     The rise of home entertainment systems such as video games, VCRs, and cheap pay TV may lower the incentives many voters once had to inform themselves.

**Personal stake in the political outcome.**     Farmers are extremely well informed about their representatives. Their livelihood depends on knowing which candidate will favor a subsidy or other forms of farm aid. Taxpayers who pay the bill on behalf of farmers are less well informed about agricultural policy because it does not pay them to figure out that two dollars of their yearly levy goes to agriculture. The gain to the majority as a whole may be large, but the gain to any one member is small. Members of such majorities have a great need to find a candidate they can trust, without incessant lobbying and application of pressure, to act as their agent.[3] The candidate they appoint collects the needed information and uses it on their behalf. In return, they may promise to vote for him and to indulge him in the use of the resources of office such as free plane rides, a large staff, and subsidized living. The politician can be someone who tells the majority, "I will inform you about the abuses of the system, but in turn I must be allowed some lesser abuses of my own."

Even though two different strategies may lead to choices of the same quality, it is important to recognize that the cost of arriving at an informed decision is not the same for everyone. It is probably true that the educated have an easier time of it and may err less in their assessment of which candidates will perform best or which issues are important. They may therefore be expected to be in possession of more information. But it is not clear how great is their advantage over other types of voters. Advances in communications technology have given a boost to organizations that specialize in analyzing information and publicizing their findings. The benefits of such specialization can be passed to uneducated voters, for whom traditionally the costs of making quality political decisions have been high.

## The Meaning of Surveys

The resources devoted to coming to a final decision, not merely some display of current interest, determine the overall quality of decision making in the electorate. A survey that shows voters following elections closely is encouraging, but one showing that voters are not up to date is not necessarily bad news. Surveys are unreliable indicators of ignorance because they report averages. Voters with high time costs may invest a larger amount of time up front before deciding to trust a candidate or advocacy group. Voters who are well educated are better at absorbing information as it comes up and may choose to be less trusting and more discerning. The educated voter may appear to be better informed than the voter with high time costs, because often he or she can be seen reading and thinking about politics, and when asked, such a voter will remember important details. But the comparison is deceptive. Each voter chooses in a way which best suits the personal circumstances. Although each may have a different style of making decisions, the quality of their decisions may not differ greatly. Both may contribute to the election of sound government.

### *Voter Knowledge and Quality of Government*

To understand the causes of ignorance and relate it to rational decision making is not to praise ignorance. Any government policy that can give voters more information is worth looking at because an informed electorate imposes discipline on its rulers. A good policy must recognize that ignorance is partially a matter of choice. Voters who are shopping around for candidates are influenced by the costs of gathering information, their own education, competing media, and their personal stake in who is elected. These parameters shape political campaigns and decide who wins office.

Some voter-information programs run by the government have the proper goal in mind but proceed on the untested assumption that flooding voters with ideas will make them more discriminating. The evidence we have suggests that gratuitous information has no lasting effect. The U.S. General Accounting Office found little evidence that voter-information activities such as announcing registration drives and registration deadlines changed people's minds on whether to vote (1990, pp. 43–48).

---

"Spending limits, which reformers praise as a way of forcing candidates to structure a sensible discussion of the issues around a modest budget, may in fact obscure the issues and harm voters."

---

Voters must be allowed to choose what they read or listen to. It may be easier and more productive to stimulate voter demand for information than to impose political education. Campaign policy can affect the cost to the voter of gathering information. Candidate advertising lowers this cost. As Patterson and McLure discovered, "The evidence clearly shows that televised network evening *newscasts* contribute almost nothing to the low interest voter's election information. . . . Televised *advertising* not only reaches low interest voters, but also teaches them useful, accurate, issue information [my emphasis]" (1976). Similarly, John G. Matsusaka and I found that in Canada campaign spending helps citizens decide whether to vote (1992b).

This suggests that spending limits, which reformers praise as a way of forcing candidates to structure a sensible discussion of the issues around a modest budget, may in fact obscure the issues and harm voters. Husted, Kenny, and Morton found that in the 1982 and 1986 Senate races incumbents spent money to divert attention from their records (1991). Challengers spent money to help constituents know what incumbents had done because, as Husted et al. explain, "the typical elected official does not adequately represent the voters and thus has a record he would like to hide from the voters." Their finding may explain why, as Bender has shown, incumbents are the strongest force behind the push for spending limits (1988). Corroborative evidence comes from Faber and Storey and many other researchers, who find that voters are likelier to remember the messages of challengers.

### Contributions, Subsidies, and Voter Information

If voters already pay attention to candidates' advertisements, does it make sense to give campaign subsidies? Subsidies may actually interfere with the transmission of information, because they obscure the size and number of contributions to the candidates. Depending on the subsidy formula, certain candidates may appear to be more popular than they truly are. This will impress voters who use opinion polls and other indices of popular opinion, such as the flow of contributions, to make up their minds. Unfortunately, the impression will be a false one.

How much a candidate spends can be just as interesting as what he says. Campaign contributions are endorsements that carry information. There is information in the *amount* of money spent on a campaign quite independent of *how* that money is spent. As Wittman writes, "Voters can also look at the list of campaign contributors (who typically make their endorsements public) and infer the characteristics of the candidates' policies (pro or con). That is, interest group endorsements are like signals in the market and provide strong cues about candidates' preferences" (1989).

An example is the candidate who buys TV ads in which only his name appears. What are voters to make of this? What information does the *act* of spending carry? Voters could infer that the candidate has the support of many private individual contributors. Each contributor can share his own insight, or his special knowledge of why the candidate is good, by giving; thus, each dollar reflects a bit of information. Hayek (1945) and later Lucas (1972) suggested that something like this happens in economic markets. The price of wheat today may reflect farmers' educated guesses about the weather next season. To a limited extent, casual observers can use the price of wheat as a signal to forecast the weather! Similarly, outside investors in the stock market may see the price of gold rising and decide to *buy* gold because the change reflects the informed bids of gold-mining specialists. Just as price may signal the quality of a stock, contributions can be a measure of the candidate.[4]

Any law which interferes with contributions, such as campaign subsidies or contribution limits, interferes with voter information.

In *Buckley v. Valeo* the Supreme Court overlooked this possibility and decided that:

> By contrast with a limitation upon expenditures for political expression, a limitation upon the amount that any one person or groups may contribute to a candidate or political committee entails only a marginal restriction upon the contributor's ability to engage in free communication. A contribution serves as a general expression of support for the candidate and his views, but does not communicate the underlying basis for the support. The quantity of communication by the contributor does not increase perceptibly with the size of his contribution, since the expression rests solely on the undifferentiated, symbolic act of contributing. At most, the size of the contribution provides a very rough index of the intensity of the contributor's support for the candidate. . . . While contributions may result in political expression if spent by a candidate . . . the transformation of contributions into political debate involves speech by someone other than the contributor (pp. 635–36).

This possible oversight by the Court is important. If contributions are really more than just "symbolic acts," the present system of contribution limits may keep information from voters. Although there is no firm evidence that contributions carry information, recent studies of how people draw information from opinion polls are suggestive. McKelvey and Ordershook showed that an uninformed voter can learn from a sequence of polls approximately where a candidate stands on some straightforward issues such as whether military spending should be $1 billion, or $2 billion, or $3 billion (1984, 1985). They tested their notions on a sample of university student volunteers convened in a laboratory for social experiments. Some of the students were told beforehand what positions the imaginary candidates held. Others were left uninformed but were paid to study the polls and figure out the positions. They found that the number of uninformed subjects who correctly identified the positions of imaginary candidates rose to 58 percent after the first poll, 79 percent after the second, and 81 percent after the third and final poll. If contributions are viewed as a form of opinion poll, then this analysis suggests that they may carry useful information and that limiting them is more than "a marginal restriction upon the contributor's ability to engage in free communication."

## The Growth of Cheap Information

Mass mailing technology, desktop publishing, and advances in marketing are key factors in the rise of public advocacy groups, policy think tanks, sophisticated trade journals, and the specialist press. These organizations process information at low cost and clarify the choices for voters.

Those who gain are consumers, taxpayers, and other loosely bound majorities. Without cheap information, they are not well placed to evaluate policies because it is too hard to distinguish the costs and benefits. As Nelson wrote, "The minority decides on the form of its gain to make it difficult for the majority to realize that it is losing as the minority gains. It is in the interests of a maximizing minority to make it hard for the majority to get information, given the crucial constraint of majority information on minority gains. . . . The minority must take its gains where the issue can be easily obscured" (1976).

For example, how many of us know that three cents of the price of every gallon of milk we buy goes to the local milk marketing board? We need the press, advocacy groups, and challenging candidates to research such hidden costs and to show us why prices are higher than they should be.[5] These technological advances threaten to alert the public to incumbents' concessions to narrow interests. Unsurprisingly, incumbents in all the Western democracies lead the movement to pass spending limits.

### Information for Those Who Need It

Information will go to those who value it most. Candidates, advocacy groups, and the media have a strong interest in directing their message to audiences who want to hear it. Phillip Nelson found that in the 1968 presidential race Democrats advertised most heavily in those areas likely to support them and that editorial positions in support of Hubert Humphrey were most frequently found in the same areas (1976). McAllister found that in the 1979 British general election, "11% of Conservative voters reported being influenced by a Conservative broadcast, but only 3% by a Labor broadcast. In 1983, voters were again more influenced by their own party's [political broadcasts]" (1985).

Candidates are better at finding their audience than in the past because they can now call on a large pool of political consultants. A president of the American Association of Political Consultants estimated that in 1988, 3,000 to 5,000 firms gave professional advice to politicians. The association itself saw its members grow from 43 in 1981 to 600 in 1988. Some estimate that politicians paid consultants $100 million in 1988. In the early days of the business, one firm would advise the candidate on all parts of a campaign. Clem Whitaker and Leone Smith Baxter were the first such consultants and prospered from the 1930s to the 1950s. Today there are people who work only on radio or television commercials or who figure the best time to run commercials. Some fundraising consultants are expert at getting small contributions. Others go for a few big catches. As consultants have specialized they have become more efficient and able to charge more for their services (*Elections '88*, 1989a, pp. 132–33).

The great advance in the ability of candidates to learn what their constituents want is not widely recognized by those who raise the alarm of high election costs. The distorted picture in the press does little to convey how far the transmission of information has come. New computer technology and the accumulated wisdom of fifty years of experience have dramatically lowered the costs of knowing and reaching an audience. An example of this advance is described by Murray Fishel, director of the Campaign Management Institute at Kent State University in the 1980s, as "interactive" campaigning. A door-to-door visit uncovers that a voter cares about a particular issue. A special computer program then scans the candidate's views on the issue and sends a letter to the concerned voter explaining the candidate's position. Other letters follow as the candidate's ideas evolve, and on election day the voter gets a call urging him or her to go to the polls (*Elections '88,* 1989a, p. 137).

The march of technology gives even the humblest of candidates the resources to organize an efficient campaign. A desktop computer system which sells for $5,000 frees campaign workers from the drudgery of managing information and allows them instead to raise money and enlist volunteers. The system can also use sophisticated but inexpensive statistical software to identify potential donors. Before the mid-1980s only mainframe computers could do this work and only wealthy candidates could afford it. This advantage has now disappeared. The situation is similar to the discovery of iron in the eleventh century B.C., which put weapons in the hands of commoners and upset the power of bronze-clad chariot aristocracies (McNeill 1963).

## Uncertainty Is Expensive

A close contest is one in which there is great uncertainty about the outcome because it is not clear which candidate is the best for the job. Voters will want to know more about the candidates in such a race than they would in a clear-cut contest between a beloved veteran incumbent and an obscure, unappealing challenger. Campaign spending in close contests responds to voter demand for information. This is why hotly contested races generate so much spending. It is not productive to lament the high cost of "overcompetitive" contests, because this is the price which must be paid to resolve uncertainty. On some questions uncertainty can persist even after the election. As Hedrick Smith writes, the "periodic paralysis [of Congress] and its brawling stalemates do not prove the incompetence or laziness of its members. Often congressional immobility reflects the lack of clear public consensus on major issues" (1988, p. 39). Spending limits may appear to lower costs, but they will lead voters to make bad choices and pay a heavier price in the long run. Only advances in the technology of communication and changes in levels of education and political interest will help voters to make better choices.

## Truth in Political Advertising

The insistence that campaigns convey useful information in convenient format may seem naive to hard-bitten election observers who believe that politicians will tell the public anything. Some skepticism is inevitable for a century in which Nazis and communists raised the political lie to an art. Lies, however, thrive in countries without competitive elections, where the incentives to be truthful are seldom strong. Western democracies generally promote honesty by allowing consumer-voters the choice of "repurchasing" the candidate at each election. Candidates are so-called experience goods. After several purchases voters will know whether they are getting what was advertised on the label and can decide to change their allegiance if unsatisfied. To paraphrase Ford, Smith, and Swasy, the behavior of politicians is influenced by the skepticism of voters (1990). If voters know when to be skeptical of advertising claims, politicians will be forced to provide them with useful information.

Ford, Smith, and Swasy find that consumers of commercial products are skeptical of claims which they can verify only after buying the product. A good political track record is deemed important for starting and continuing a congressional or presidential career (Nelson 1976), a sign that previous consumers (voters) have sampled the political product to their satisfaction. Many novice candidates for Congress present themselves only after extended tours of duty in political outposts such as city councils, school boards, and Kiwanis clubs. The reputations they establish there soothe the anxious voter poised to commit himself to a full term under a single representative.

Once a politician is elected one lie can erode the work of years, whereas being honest and keeping promises will generate further political capital. The presence of competitors and press, eager to ferret out unbecoming and sensational facts, may keep all but the crookedest candidates in line. In addition, dishonest candidates may not thrive because parties have an incentive to choose representatives who will not embarrass them. A scandal such as Watergate can harm a party long after the culprits have retired to writing their memoirs.

Even if politicians do lie, voters may be well equipped to see through the falsehood or to deal with biased reports. Soviet citizens expertly divined truth from official balderdash, and Westerners are capable of similar insights, as Wittman describes: "I have never met anyone who believes that the Defense Department does not exaggerate the need for defense procurement. But if everyone knows that the Defense Department will exaggerate the importance of its contributions to human welfare, then, on average, voters will sufficiently discount the Defense Department claims. Hence biased sources of information need not lead to biases in belief" (1989).

None of this proves that election campaigns will be forums of sincere and honest discussion. It is not clear how constrained politicians are from bending the truth. But there are indications that voters are not lambs in need of constant government guidance.


## Let Voters Have Information

Candidates and constituents can learn about each other in many ways. Understanding how the two exchange information helps us see who benefits or loses from spending and contribution limits, publicly sponsored voter information programs, and free airtime laws. Such initiatives may in fact leave voters with less information than they had before. Public policy should allow voters to choose their own means of informing themselves. Candidates have strong incentives to provide information where it is most demanded, and voters have many ways of collecting that information. Image advertising is a much belittled but efficient means of compressing complicated messages into comprehensible form and may be of as much value in making an intelligent choice between candidates as issue advertising. Voters can also inform themselves in ways that do not register clearly in surveys designed to measure how up-to-date people are on the issues. Instead of paying attention day-by-day to political campaigns, some voters may invest time in finding a group or candidate they can trust to sift through the information for them. These voters may not *appear* to be well informed but this is because they have delegated the task to information specialists they trust.

The quality of people's political choices determines the quality of the government they get. Governments have never been good at maintaining a high quality in the goods they purchase and produce. There is no reason to believe they can do any better in the regulation of politics. In the end it is not government-sponsored voter information programs or subsidies to candidates that will help people make sound political choices. It is the natural determinants of the demand and supply of information that will leave the greatest mark. Demand has much to do with education. Supply is driven by technological advances. The advance of technology will give an advantage to outsiders, allowing them to successfully challenge incumbents. The result will be more political competition.

# 4

# *Who Benefits from Spending Limits?*

One thing is clear: The only meaningful way to reform Senate elections is to have limits on campaign spending.

George J. Mitchell, *Senate Democratic leader*

An absolute, fixed cap on campaign spending is nothing more than a prescription for incumbency protection.

Bob Dole, *Senate Republican leader*

FOR MOST OF THIS CENTURY doctors and lawyers did not allow members of their professions to advertise. This protected established practitioners from eager young competitors. In congressional politics, incumbents have tried but never managed to stifle advertising. The vigilance of the Supreme Court, and disputes on the House and Senate floors over details which might help Democrats more than Republicans, have denied elected representatives the protection they so actively seek. Today there are no spending limits on congressional campaigns and only voluntary limits on presidential candidates who accept public subsidies for their campaigns.

It seems strange and contrary to argue that members of Congress need protection and that they should seek it in a spending limit. In 1992 voters returned 88.5 percent of their incumbent senators seeking reelection and 93.1 percent of House representatives. Members of Congress are awash with money which they flaunt to dissuade serious challengers from running (Cobb 1988). How could spending limits do anything but *harm* incumbents? Reform groups make this apparent imbalance of power their theme and have long tried to convince the public that campaign spending corrupts democracy by entrenching the established powers. Incumbents have been in power too long, and spending limits are the way to chasten or remove them.

Superstitions like these cloud the debate on spending limits, because it is hard to measure the quality of government. How can we know whether an incumbent takes good care of his constituents or whether Congress works hard for the people? A popular method is to gauge government's output by its input. Long-term incumbents who spend fortunes on reelection trouble some observers. The problem with this view is that it lacks perspective; it does not distinguish between a long term that stifles competition and a long term that reflects a happy constituency. It sees good and bad incumbents as the same and holds them as examples of the uncompetitiveness of American elections.

It is more pertinent to ask whether a campaign law stops challengers from contesting incumbents. An incumbent who is contested will have to answer to criticism. He or she may be returned to office many times but only if the candidate is prepared to bend to challenger attacks and respond to the moods of constituents. Hitler banned all criticism and ruled at his whim for twelve years. Roosevelt also governed for twelve years but in the service of his people. The difference lay in that Roosevelt had to answer public criticisms. He had no spending limit behind which to hide.

The incumbent's fear of criticism is well founded. Even though incumbents are better at raising money, their money does not go as far because voters are more receptive to challenger messages. What challengers spend in elections wins them more votes than the money that incumbents spend. With each advance in communication technology challengers become a bigger threat. Spending limits can undo the challengers' advantage and spare incumbents the effort of raising funds.

Congress has often tried to pass spending limits in the wake of political scandals. The great campaign reforms of 1974 followed

Watergate. The limits and subsidies which were passed in 1992 but vetoed by President Bush grew out of the Keating Five scandal and the scandals at the House bank and post office (Donovan 1992). In both cases incumbents explained that the proposed laws would promote competition in elections by ensuring that the richest candidates could not spend their way into office. These laws would work in the public interest by allowing any citizen with good ideas to run for election without fear of losing to the wealth of an opponent.

Abrams and Settle have criticized this public interest view on the grounds that regulations which appear to protect one group (voters) may actually be written for the benefit of a different group (politicians): "Rational, self-interested individuals, groups, or industries seek regulation as a means of serving their own private interests. . . . When regulation has the potential for directly affecting the legislators themselves (e.g., political campaign regulations), the economic approach suggests that the regulation would be designed to serve the legislators' interest rather than some vaguely defined 'public interest' " (1978).

The economic approach to which the authors refer is that of George Stigler, who argued that "every industry or occupation that has enough political power to utilize the state will seek to control entry" (1971). In economic markets existing firms can charge consumers higher prices by restricting the entry of competitors. When applied to political markets, this approach suggests that, contrary to popular opinion, spending limits can make it harder to enter politics. Legislators may exploit popular fears about the use of money in elections to pass laws that make it difficult for challengers to compete.

Under certain circumstances limits may benefit incumbents by increasing their vote margins and consequently their hold on power. This extra power can make it easier for incumbents to act in their own narrow interests to the detriment of the majority. Certain categories of spending, such as volunteer labor, may be exempt and may heavily favor incumbents from the party which relies most on volunteers. Allied regulation governing how campaign resources may and may not be used can affect competition as much as the simple limits themselves do.

This chapter gives the history of spending limits in U.S. elections and explains who benefits from limits. I review the law which Congress passed in 1992 and explain why President Bush vetoed it. Under the law, any eligible candidate accepting public subsidies bound himself to a loose spending limit. The limit would have risen in response to heavy spending by an opponent who did not accept subsidies. This awkward compromise between freedom of speech and censorship was forced on Congress by the Supreme Court in its 1976 decision in the case of *Buckley v. Valeo*. Congress is constantly probing the boundaries of this ruling and may one day pass more ambitious self-protection laws. I describe what shape these might take and why they should be resisted. In particular I warn that Congress may eventually try to restrict what single-issue groups can say during elections. I also emphasize throughout that limits actually raise the cost of elections. Candidates waste resources looking for legal loopholes in the law, and loophole spending is an inefficient way of reaching voters.

## The Power of Challenger Spending

Reformers paint the past fifteen years as a bleak period in the history of Congress; a period during which incumbents reigned unchallenged. Their strongest evidence is that incumbents for the House have been reelected roughly 90 percent of the time and that senators have been reelected with slightly less frequency. Taking such statistics out of context does not make it easier to decide whether we need tighter regulations. Between 1978 and 1988 only nine of thirty-two winning congressional challengers needed to outspend the incumbent in order to oust him or her. In 1986 six Democratic challengers defeated Republican incumbents without outspending them. Five of the six challengers were outspent by a million dollars or more and four were outspent by a ratio of 2:1 (Congressional Quarterly Guide, Fall 1990, p. 12). In the 1990 campaign, many incumbents won only by slim margins against challengers who spent little to oppose them. One challenger dressed in a dark-horse costume to dramatize how little money he had and took 47 percent of the vote against House majority leader Richard Gephardt (Cook 1991, p. 141).

Such statistics suggest that federal elections are more competitive than many pretend. Since candidates started reporting their spending twenty years ago, academics have been exploring the advantages of incumbents and challengers. Two findings emerge from their diverse efforts.

---

"Legislators may exploit popular fears about the use of money in elections to pass laws that make it difficult for challengers to compete."

---

First, incumbents start a campaign with a large block of committed voters. Kristian S. Palda and I estimated that being a first-term incumbent in Canadian parliamentary elections was worth an extra 8,100 votes (in districts with roughly 50,000 constituents). Longer-term incumbents started out their races with a 12,200 vote advantage over their challengers (1985).

The second finding is that challenger spending is more potent. Jacobson (1978, 1985) found that in 1974 House elections challengers gained on average 12.1 percent of the vote for every $100,000 they spent, whereas incumbents gained only 2.8 percent (1985). He found similar results for congressional elections in the early 1980s. Abramowitz has confirmed these results in a study of Senate elections spanning the period from 1974 to 1986 (1988). In particular he found that of the many factors which can influence an election, "the challenger's campaign spending is by far the most important factor differentiating winning from losing incumbents: almost 30% of the difference in support between winning and losing incumbents is directly attributable to the challenger's campaign spending."[1]

These two findings are the first step toward understanding who benefits from limits. Incumbents' use of franked mailing rights, paid travel, and government office staff to promote themselves while in office assures them of a large block of initial voter support but leaves little to be accomplished by campaign spending. Challenger spending is a threat to incumbents because challengers have not spent to the point where their money loses its power. A limit could protect the initial vote advantage of incumbents while saving them the expense of a pitched campaign.

Incumbents try to balance the costs of fundraising against the extra votes this money gets them. Although money may buy votes, it is unpleasant to raise. As Hubert Humphrey exclaimed, fundraising is a "dirty, demeaning, disgusting business" (Orren 1979). A ceiling on campaign spending may lower the incumbent's chances of winning, but it would also save him or her a great deal of money. Incumbents may willingly sacrifice votes to gain time away from fundraising and to avoid the obligation to donors that comes with accepting contributions. An incumbent who can stomach risk and is not afraid to cut things close will find profit in the trade of votes for convenience.

We cannot assert without question that limits are incumbent-protection laws.[2] Their effect depends on the severity of the limits, the potency of challenger spending, and the initial incumbent advantage. There is, however, some evidence that in practice incumbents set limits low enough to protect themselves. In a subtle study, Bender found that members of Congress for whom campaign spending was not a powerful getter of votes were likely to support amendments to the Federal Election Campaign Act restricting spending (1988). Others have put the argument more forcefully, including Gary Jacobson, the dean of statistical inquiries into the power of money in elections: "Restrictions on money contributed to or spent by candidates have the effect of limiting competition and thus favoring those already at the top of the competitive heap—the incumbents. Indeed, in forming campaign finance policy, Congress has consistently operated as, to borrow Mayhew's phrase, 'a cross-party conspiracy of incumbents to keep their jobs.'" (Jacobson 1979).[3]

## Do Subsidies Make Elections More Competitive?

If spending limits can be good for incumbents, then spending limits and campaign subsidies together may be even better. Reform enthusiasts prefer to believe that subsidies give "underfunded" challengers a boost and make elections more competitive. As Adamany writes, "Public financing can assure sufficient campaign funds to stimulate competitive elections even as campaign finance regulations diminish the role of large private contributions" (1990, p. 111). Such broad statements are an example of the current lack of perspective in the campaign finance debate. Just as spending limits may not always benefit incumbents, subsidies may not always benefit challengers. If the spending limit is too low, a subsidy will not help the challenger win. At best it will relieve both the challenger and the incumbent of the trouble of raising money. Canada, the United Kingdom, France, and Italy all combine subsidies with limits in a way which leaves little doubt about who benefits. In Canada, the parties get subsidies in proportion to how much money they raised in the previous election. Incumbent parties usually raise more money, and collect greater subsidies.

In the United States, subsidies *must* in practice go with spending limits. In *Buckley v. Valeo* the Supreme Court equated spending in elections with freedom of speech. Spending-limit proposals offer candidates incentives to participate voluntarily. Presidential candidates have received subsidies and stuck to limits since 1976. There are no spending limits in Congress, but every proposal for voluntary limits since *Buckley* has offered subsidies to candidates who keep their spending down. Senate Resolution 3 gave eligible candidates (those who raised above a threshold level of contributions) cheap postage and vouchers to spend on television ads, as well as "contingency" money to protect them against candidates who did not take subsidies and spent beyond the limit. House Resolution 3750, which came out at the same time, was similar to S3. In May of 1993 President Bill Clinton revived the proposals for television and postage vouchers for candidates who volunteered to limit their spending. The White House estimated the plan would cost $75 million each year in public subsidies for the vouchers.

Many incumbents do not like this arrangement of voluntary limits and subsidies because it is less effective than a mandatory limit. The arrangement would relieve them of some of the duties of fundraising but would not protect them from well-financed challengers who passed up the benefits and ignored the limits. Some incumbents have tried to impose mandatory limits by amending the Constitution to get around the Supreme Court's ruling that limits violate freedom of speech. In 1988 Democratic

Senator Earnest Hollings proposed the following amendment (Senate Joint Resolution 282):

> Section 1. Congress shall have power to set limits on campaign expenditures by, in support of, or in opposition to any candidate in any primary or other election for Federal office.
>     Section 2. The States shall have power to set limits on campaign expenditures by, in support of, or in opposition to any candidate in any primary or other election for State or local office.

Hollings's reason for proposing the amendment was that "elections are supposed to be contests of ideas. . . . [Instead] they degenerate into megadollar derbies" (Cloud 1988, p. 1108). Hearings on the amendment were held but when the bill went to the Senate floor for a vote, Republicans filibustered and there were too few votes for cloture (Magelby and Nelson 1990, p. 166). In 1992 Hollings continued his efforts with Senate Joint Resolution 35, which was identical to Senate Joint Resolution 282. A constitutional amendment is unlikely because it would take two-thirds of the House and the Senate to approve. As long as Republicans are strongly against limits, this sort of legislative measure will not work.

## So What If Limits Help Incumbents?

With so many congressional incumbents apparently firmly entrenched in a system that works well for them, it seems strange that many should want to change that system by introducing spending limits. Alexander and Bauer point out that the rise in congressional campaign spending is due almost entirely to incumbents spending more. Incumbents now face for the most part "token" challengers who are "obscure and ill funded" (1991, p. 54). Turnover is low and is due mostly to the death or retirement of incumbents. How could a spending limit possibly help these well-funded incumbents who sweep aside all opposition with their impressive resources?

In posing such questions supporters of limits appear to be on their firmest ground, and anyone who suspects that long terms in office are a sign that politics is not competitive cannot help being impressed by their arguments. I would maintain, however, that spending limits can be in the interest of a near-permanent house of incumbents and that limits entrench incumbents and help them to win by large margins. This gives them security and allows them to carry on in office less constrained by public opinion. We should not judge Congress by its age but by how alert it is to constituent needs.

### Public Servant, Public Master

How long incumbents stay in power says little about how beholden they are to special interests or efficiently they will serve their constituents. Most politicians come to office with an agenda of things they would like to accomplish, but it is never easy to mesh those ideas with the demands of a changing constituency. A politician can stay in office a long and miserable time if he or she is always ready to please constituents by borrowing the closest challenger's policies. In the 1992 presidential primaries President Bush's policies became more conservative to meet a dangerous challenge for the Republican nomination from Pat Buchanan. Although Buchanan had little money or volunteer help, his ideas appealed to the vocal conservative wing of the party. Bush might have changed paths even without a Buchanan on his heels, but he would have done so at his own pace. Democratic House leader Richard Gephardt's share of his district's vote fell from 63 percent in 1988 to 57 percent in 1990 because constituents believed he was more interested in partisan politics and national issues than in the problems at home in his own district. Both Bush and Gephardt adapted, but some incumbents prefer not to adapt and simply retire. In 1992 many House members retired out of "frustration over having become the whipping boy of the news media and the public" (Katz 1992, p. 851).[4] The academic support for these real-world examples is a study by Alan Abramowitz which found that House incumbents who were most successful at keeping their seats were the ones who tried to please their constituents by frequently crossing party lines. According to Abramowitz, "a representative who voted with the opposing party 100% of the time would have added almost 10 percentage points to his margin over the challenger compared with the margin he would have received if he had voted strictly along party lines" (1991).

These examples suggest that political competition is more than just a rapid turnover of those in charge. In economic markets the existence of competition is seldom measured by how many years the main producers have been in business or by the longevity of managers and entrepreneurs, and the tradition of classifying a market with only one large producer as anticompetitive is fading. Instead, competition is now thought to depend on how easily competitors can enter the race. In a competitive market producers cannot manipulate the rules to earn profit above the rewards due their natural abilities. A monopoly is not competitive because it can earn abnormal profits by keeping potential rivals out, usually with the help of government, as in the case of American Telephone and Telegraph's monopoly. Competition is likely to be healthy in markets where each producer can contest the other's price. It is not necessary that there be many producers—even one may do—or that new producers enter the market regularly. All that is required is for each to know that any attempt to raise the price for abnormal profit at the consumer's expense will result in the challenge of a lower price by another producer and the possible loss of some share of the established firm's market.

In 1990 many congressional incumbents lost a significant share of their constituency "markets" to challengers. Roughly 85 percent of House incumbents were reelected with less than 60 percent of the vote, which was twice the number in that category in 1988 (Congressional Quarterly Guide, Spring 1991, p. 3). The fall in incumbent vote-shares sent a strong message that voters were not pleased with their representatives. The "kick the bums out" movement that was predicted did not materialize, but the swing against incumbents showed that incumbents do not rule over an acquiescent populace and that voters have ways to show they are not pleased.

### Political Competition

A more formal definition of electoral competition can help us make concrete statements about reform proposals. Economist Gary Becker used the idea of politics as a market to define political competition: "In an ideal democracy competition is free in the sense that no appreciable costs or artificial barriers prevent an individual from running for office and from putting a platform before the electorate" (1958). This perspective differs from the more common perception, well described by Ferejohn, that competition is free and at its height when electoral contests are close and when there is high candidate turnover (1977).

When Becker-style competition is absent politicians have a strong incentive to profit from their positions at the expense of constituents. Profit may come from striking secret deals with special interests or simply from attending to business other than that of governing. Campaign money promotes competition by allowing challengers to advertise these flaws. Voters count on such information because the costs to any given individual of researching political abuses is higher than the benefits. Winning office is incentive enough for challengers to raise funds and to communicate what they know about the incumbent to the public. Campaign spending lowers the costs to voters of making an informed choice. Incumbents who are faced with an informed electorate have a strong incentive to change their policies to resemble those of popular challengers. The final result may be a Congress full of old but adaptable incumbents. Otherwise, as Stigler argued, if one party becomes extortionate, or badly mistakes what voters want, "it is possible to elect another party which will provide the governmental services at a price more closely proportioned to the costs of the party" (1971).

In adapting concepts of economic competition to politics, many differences between economics and politics must be kept in mind. Stigler noted that the market analogy is not perfect because the channels of political decision making are "gross or filtered or noisy." In politics many people must decide at once, making voting on specific issues very costly and forcing voters to "eschew direct expressions of marginal changes in preferences." In other words, one does not get exactly what one would like to buy in politics. Stigler believed, however, that the analogy is close enough to conclude that "if a political party has monopoly control over the governmental machine, one might expect that it could collect most of the benefits of regulation for itself."

## Barriers to Entry

Political competition protects against a primary role for money in deciding who wins an election. Millionaires, or candidates who get their money from millionaires, cannot simply buy their way into office and then do as they please. If the issues being debated are important to voters, and if voters are dissatisfied with their leaders, candidates who are poor will be able to raise money. Provided they have popular support, these challengers will not need to advertise as much as incumbents to win.

The ability of poorly funded politicians and interest groups to win elections and referendums on important questions is widely documented. Republicans were reminded of how ineffective money can be in a string of elections between 1982 and 1990. Their national committee spent $304 million to elect federal candidates, whereas the Democratic committee spent only $56 million. But in each election the Republicans lost at least one congressional seat. Why did this happen? Perhaps because money is not the only answer to winning elections. There are many forces that interact subtly with spending. Is the candidate female, an incumbent, a good speaker? Is the con-stituency wealthy, educated, religious? A female candidate might spend a fortune in a traditional district and get nowhere, or she might spend little in a liberal-minded district and do quite well. Hard work and organization can make up for a candidate's shortage of money. In fact, as Herbert Alexander wrote, "Voters sometimes refuse to respond favorably to frills, blitz campaigns, or wealthy candidates, creating a backlash that may turn voters off" (1984, p. 21).

### Franking and Other Privileges

Problems with competition do not start when candidates are rich. Problems start when candidates get a monopoly over campaign resources. In private markets, monopolies do not last long without government help. In politics the same may be true. Government can help incumbents establish, if not a monopoly, then at least an advantage in campaign resources by granting franking privileges. This privilege entitles representatives to send newsletters and questionnaires to their constituents. As Table 1 and Figure 5 show, the value of congressional franked mailing can be almost as great as the amount all candidates, both challenger and incumbent, spend in a two-year election cycle. In the 1991 debate on franking privileges Republican members

TABLE 1
Franked Mail Sent by Congress, 1972–1989

|  | Franking costs (in thousands of 1992 dollars) | Thousands of pieces of congressional mail | Franking costs per eligible voter (in 1992 dollars) | Pieces of mail per eligible voter | Franking costs divided by congressional campaign spending |
|---|---|---|---|---|---|
| 1972 | 109,165 | 308,900 | 0.78 | 2.2 | 0.43 |
| 1973 | 66,118 | 310,600 | 0.47 | 2.2 | — |
| 1974 | 85,562 | 321,000 | 0.61 | 2.3 | 0.35 |
| 1975 | 99,628 | 312,400 | 0.69 | 2.2 | — |
| 1976 | 179,150 | 561,300 | 1.22 | 3.8 | 0.64 |
| 1977 | 107,044 | 293,300 | 0.72 | 2.0 | — |
| 1978 | 103,781 | 430,200 | 0.68 | 2.8 | 0.25 |
| 1979 | 123,717 | 409,900 | 0.80 | 2.7 | — |
| 1980 | 85,107 | 511,300 | 0.54 | 3.3 | 0.21 |
| 1981 | 79,166 | 395,600 | 0.49 | 2.5 | — |
| 1982 | 107,624 | 771,800 | 0.65 | 4.7 | 0.22 |
| 1983 | 129,360 | 556,800 | 0.77 | 3.3 | — |
| 1984 | 156,258 | 924,600 | 0.92 | 5.4 | 0.31 |
| 1985 | 110,277 | 675,000 | 0.64 | 3.9 | — |
| 1986 | 120,651 | 758,700 | 0.70 | 4.4 | 0.21 |
| 1987 | 111,204 | 494,700 | 0.63 | 2.8 | — |
| 1988 | 95,973 | 804,900 | 0.54 | 4.5 | 0.18 |
| 1989 | 95,096 | 598,600 | 0.53 | 3.3 | — |

Dash = not applicable.
Sources: FEC press releases; Ornstein et al., 1992, pp. 139, 160; U.S. Department of Commerce. Statistical Abstract of the United States, 1992, 1989, 1984, 1981, 1977 issues; U.S. Department of Commerce. Survey of Current Business, March 1993.

of Congress pointed out that the $130 million that House members spent on franking in 1991 was more than twice what all House challengers spent for all parts of their campaigns in the 1990 elections (Donovan 1992).

Figure 6 shows that congressional mailings reach a peak in election years. This of course suggests that members of Congress use their privilege in part to help themselves get reelected. More direct evidence comes from a Common Cause study which interviewed Senate staff in the early 1980s and found that over one-third of the Senate was using official funds and sophisticated direct-mail techniques to promote reelection. As one staffer remarked, "The frank isn't a loophole, it is a black hole. If you can't do it under the frank, you're either dumb or hopelessly unsubtle" (Franzitch 1982, pp. 174–76).

FIGURE 5
## Franked Mailing Privileges as a Fraction of Congressional Campaign Spending Over Two-Year Election Cycles, 1972–1988

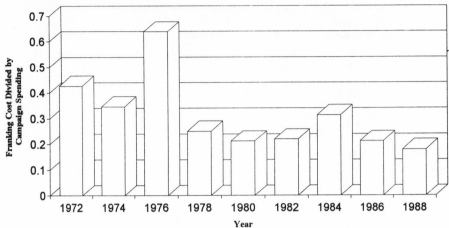

*Sources:* FEC press releases; Ornstein et al., 1992, p. 139.

FIGURE 6
## Pieces of Franked Mail per Eligible Voter, 1972–1989

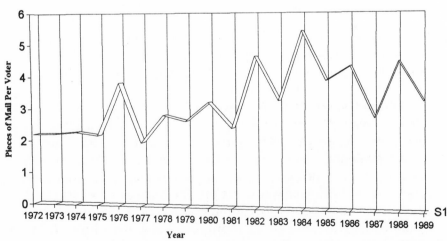

*Sources:* Ornstein et al., 1992, p. 160; U.S. Department of Commerce. *Statistical Abstract of the United States,* 1992.

Free mail is not the only advantage incumbents receive. Government also pays for their staff, research, and travel, all of which may be used to run a continuous campaign between elections. The value of all these government resources is difficult to estimate. In a recent attempt, Carter and Racine asked how many votes a dollar of franking and other privileges bought a candidate relative to a dollar raised through contributions, which the candidate was free to spend any way he wished (1990). They calculated that in the early 1980s, over an election cycle, the frank and other advantages were worth $0.55 per capita in campaign dollars, or a little over $200,000 (in 1982 dollars) to the average congressional incumbent.[5]

---

"Free mail is not the only advantage incumbents receive. Government also pays for their staff, research, and travel, all of which may be used to run a continuous campaign between elections."

---

It is not clear how serious a barrier franking privileges are to challengers. Challengers may be able to catch up with incumbents if they are allowed to spend as much as they wish to get their message across. Without spending limits, franking privileges may be just a useless taxpayer expense and little else. But operating simultaneously with spending limits that prevent challengers from campaigning as hard as they would wish, the franking privilege may give incumbents a real advantage.

### "Loose Cannons": Spending by Single-Issue Groups and Independent Candidates

Candidates from the major parties are not the only ones to spend money during an election. Individuals and PACs also advertise what they think, irritating and worrying the major parties and making themselves targets of reform. To anyone who supports candidate spending limits, limits on independent groups seem natural and necessary. Candice Nelson summarizes the prevalent view: independent groups are unaccountable and may not even be independent (1990). Some form of control is needed to protect the public from false advertising and to prevent candidates from getting around their contribution limits by riding the coattails of independent group spending.

A widely publicized example of how candidates can benefit from money spent by independents is the 1988 presidential campaign of Vice President George Bush. During the campaign two independent conservative groups bought ads that questioned Democratic presidential candidate George Dukakis's record on crime. Although the ads were placed without Bush's guidance, they may have won him votes (Alexander 1991). By mounting campaigns of their own, independent groups can help a presidential candidate receive more attention than he could obtain on his own. Independent spending is also a way around contribution limits. Instead of giving directly to a candidate, a group may instead support that candidate by advertising on his behalf. This form of indirect support is not subject to a limit, provided the group does not coordinate its activities with the candidate. Many reformers believe that this dark avenue for money may lead us back to the pre-1971 era when legend has it that money blatantly bought government favors.

Unfortunately, those who defend independent spending against such arguments do so on the grounds that a limit would violate the First and Fourteenth Amendments' guarantees of free speech. This line of defense may appeal to our deep convictions that people should be allowed to express themselves. But critics of independent spending should be answered on less metaphysical grounds. A case for free independent spending should try to explain what concrete benefits voters get from such spending. I want to argue that independent groups serve voters in ways that parties no longer can: by providing them with detailed political information and by organizing campaigns around single issues. They should also be recognized as a new device Americans can use to keep their leaders responsive.

### Are "Independent" Groups Really Independent?

One reason independent spenders are looked on as the tools of politicians is that, since they blossomed in the late 1970s, most of their support has gone to incumbents (Magelby and Nelson

1990). These reported allegiances are deceptive because by and large independent groups are not good at cooperating or striking deals with anyone. They worry the two major parties because they are unpredictable and they even distress candidates on whose behalf they advertise. As a former campaign manager said, "Independent expenditure scares the daylights out of me. A third party comes in that doesn't know my strategy or my budget and interjects itself. This could terribly jeopardize a campaign" (Sabato 1985, pp. 102–3). A congressional aide referred to independent campaigns as "loose cannons on deck," and Republican senator Dan Evans, on whose behalf such a group had campaigned in 1983, said, "I think unquestionably if you measured campaigning by sleaze factor, that independent expenditures on campaigns are probably the highest sleaze factor in campaigns today" (Novak and Cobb 1987, p. 35). The sleaze factor can offend the voters it is meant to win over. In the 1982 Senate race in Maryland where the National Conservative PAC maligned Senator Paul Sarbanes, the conservative group's excesses actually helped him raise money from liberal supporters whom the ads had offended, according to Magelby and Nelson (1990).

### Congress versus the Courts

What looks like cooperation or support from independent groups is often an unwelcome interference in the incumbent's campaign. Congress tried to tie down the loose cannons in 1974 by limiting to $1,000 per year what any group or individual could spend on promoting or opposing a candidate. Their intention was to stop candidates from getting around their own spending limits by having independents spend for them. The Supreme Court ruled that this violated the First and Fourteenth Amendments' guarantees on free speech because "a restriction on the amount of money a person or group can spend on political communication during a campaign necessarily reduces the quantity of expression by restricting the number of issues discussed, the depth of their exploration, and the size of the audience reached. This is because virtually every means of communicating ideas in today's mass society requires the expenditure of money" (*Buckley v. Valeo*, p. 643). The Court added that "being free to engage in political expression subject to a ceiling on expenditures is like being free to drive an automobile as far and often as one desires on a single tank of gasoline" (*Buckley v. Valeo*, p. 643).

Laws and regulations coming after *Buckley v. Valeo* further established that independent groups may spend all they wish but that their spending must be made without any input from the candidate or his committee. If there is input, the spending is treated as a contribution to the candidate and is subject to contribution limits. In 1985 in *Federal Election Commission v. National Conservative Political Action Committee*, for example, the court struck down U.S.C. 9012(f), which forbade independent PACs from spending on behalf of presidential candidates who had accepted federal subsidies.

The Court also worked to remove more subtle barriers which the 1974 Federal Election Campaign Act had put in the way of independents having a say in elections. The law forbade corporations and unions from contributing or campaigning with "treasury money" (profits or union dues) (United States Code [U.S.C.] 441b). The law did not distinguish, however, between profit and nonprofit corporations. This meant that nonprofit corporations could not use their charitable earnings to contribute to candidates or to campaign for them. Treasury funds could be used only in a limited way to solicit contributions for the group's PAC, a practice which imposed significant administrative costs on charitable organizations. In the 1986 case *Federal Election Commission v. Massachusetts Citizens for Life* the Supreme Court removed this restriction on nonprofit corporations in order to spare these corporations the administrative costs that many small entities might not be able to bear. The Court was satisfied that the reporting requirements of U.S.C. 434(c) could meet the state's interest in disclosure of contributions "in a manner less restrictive than imposing the full panoply of regulations that accompany status as a political committee" (p. 262).

As independent spending grew in the 1980s, Congress looked for ways to sweep aside *Buckley v. Valeo* and its legacy. Three senators—most notably Democrat Ernest Hollings—introduced constitutional amendments to directly overturn *Buckley,* and Democratic senator Timothy E. Wirth tried to convince the Supreme Court to reconsider its decision (Novak and Cobb 1987). After both efforts failed Congress enacted special public funding for candidates facing attacks by independent groups. Senate Resolution 3, passed in 1992 but vetoed by President Bush, would have given senatorial candidates a dollar for each dollar above the first ten thousand dollars which independents spent against them. The law also forced independent spenders to advise broadcasters of the names of the candidates against whom their advertising was directed. Broadcasters would then have been obliged to pass this information on to targeted candidates and allow them to buy time immediately after the independent ad. The accompanying House Resolution 3750 was similar but went even further by forbidding party committees, as well as any PACs registered as lobbyists such as the National Rifle Association or the American Medical Association, from advertising during elections.

The House Resolution probably would have been ruled unconstitutional, but the fact that the House was willing to taunt the Supreme Court shows how irritating independent spending is to members of Congress. A memorable display of such irritation took place in 1986 when Democratic representative Fortney "Pete" Stark called the leaders of the American Medical Association "troglodytes" and ignored their pleas to increase Medicare payments to doctors. Stark expected no serious challenge to his incumbency and was surprised when the American Medical PAC spent $252,000 to help his challenger, David Williams. Williams did not win, but such an incident can put pressure on incumbents to consider competing views on how to govern.

Official hostility toward independent groups was also evident in President Bill Clinton's 1993 proposals for election reform. His plan relied heavily on giving candidates subsidies in return for their agreement to limit campaign spending. Obedient candidates who faced attacks from opponents who took no federal subsidy would have their spending limit raised. If these obedient candidates became the target of more than $10,000 in independent group spending they would receive extra "communication vouchers" from the federal government. In addition, broadcast stations would be required to make time available immediately after the independent broadcast for the candidate to respond.

### Fairness and Accountability

Another argument against independent spending is that it allows groups with money who are not accountable to anyone to change how people vote and to corrupt politicians. Opponents of independent spending paint elections as a form of class warfare in which the wealth of some candidates unduly distorts the election process. In a political system which grants rights to everybody, advantage should not be allowed to accrue to those who have means. Hence those who believe they are disadvantaged—usually incumbents struggling against angry independent spenders—also like to believe they need subsidies and protective laws.

The problem, to paraphrase the legal scholar Bruno Leoni (1991), is that all the attempts at integrating political freedom with economic freedom make it impossible to grant everybody freedom, conceived as the absence of constraint exercised by other people. Introducing freedom from want into a political or legal system leads to a new concept of freedom which differs from the old notion that freedom is the absence of constraint. This new concept of freedom gives the state an excuse to equalize resources or limit independent spending in the name of fairness and to slow down popular movements.

The Supreme Court has treated the idea of fairness delicately. In *Buckley v. Valeo* it explained the problems with fairness. "The concept that government may restrict the speech of some elements of our society in order to enhance the relative voice of others is wholly foreign to the First Amendment, which was designed 'to secure the widest possible dissemination of information from diverse and antagonistic sources.' . . . *The First Amendment's protection against government abridgement of free expression cannot properly be made to depend on a person's financial ability to engage in public discussion* [my emphasis]" (*Buckley v. Valeo,* p. 649). The Court, however, tempered this view by upholding that profitable corporations and labor unions should not be allowed to use their treasury funds (profits or union dues) to contribute or to campaign. In *Federal Election Commission v. Massachusetts Citizens for Life* the Court repeated its long-standing position that "resources amassed in the economic marketplace" can be used to obtain "an unfair advantage in the political marketplace" (p. 257).

The *Massachusetts* case shows how tightly fairness is tangled with the notion of accountability. The Court believes it is fair for a corporation to advertise from a segregated fund because such advertising is an indication of popular support for the corporation's political ideas. In contrast, resources in the treasury of the corporation "reflect the economically motivated decisions of investors and customers. The availability of these resources may make the corporation a formidable political presence, even though the power of the corporation may be no reflection of the power of its ideas" (p. 258). In the first case the corporation is judged to be accountable to part of the electorate: its employees and shareholders. In the second case it acts out of narrow greed and uses corporate profits to gain an unfair political advantage.

The Court's between-the-lines support of accountability seems a reasonable requirement of any group that spends money in an attempt to influence the public. It reflects the fairly widespread view that "with no sponsoring organization to accept responsibility, and with contributors scattered across the country, those who make direct independent expenditures may be tempted to engage in activities that verge on excess" (Twentieth Century Fund Task Force 1984, p. 4). Democratic senator Paul Sarbanes put it more bluntly: "The independent PACs operate outside of [a] framework of accountability and simply become hit artists on the political scene" (Alexander and Haggerty 1981, p. 157). These views, however, are not as reasonable or obvious as they seem. They are based on a distorted idea of how independent groups operate and an exaggerated impression of the power of money in elections.

Official accountability is not necessary for balanced, informative elections. What matters is whether every argument can be contested. Money is most likely to cloud the issues and mislead voters when competitors are forbidden to express their views. Money by itself does not buy elections. Many PACs have attacked candidates to little effect because voters simply did not like or believe what they said, or because voters believed that the interests such groups represented were too narrow. Several important failures by the National Conservative PAC and the American-Israeli PAC in the 1980s support this point, as do the lavish but unsuccessful presidential campaigns of conspiracy theorist Lyndon Larouche. PACs and other independent spenders may fail precisely because they are not accountable. How strongly the public believes a message depends in part on the consequences of lying. A group that is not accountable will suffer less damage from being discovered in a lie than one that is accountable, which is why people trust the former less.

Campaigns by independent groups that have gained the public's trust can increase the flow of information in elections. The great advantage of such groups is that they can focus attention on one issue, which major parties cannot afford to do. The specialized function of single-issue groups is a major political innovation which promises to increase competition in elections. Independent groups can be used as agents for the public, collecting money and using it in a disciplined way to keep politicians in line. Some ideas have too little support for a party to embrace, or are too fleeting to found a party on. Because independent groups have low setup costs, and no need to please the majority on a large number of issues, they are well suited to promote such ideas. When loyal supporters of the large parties have a complaint, they can send a message to their leaders at low cost through a single-issue group. Even moderate voters can use committed groups to their own advantage. This positive function of independents has been largely ignored in the reform debate, which may explain the almost paranoid, unsubstantiated fear that wealthy, unaccountable interests will gain too much political power.

### Save the Parties!

Independent groups can be expected to grow as the costs of organizing members and informing voters fall. This may make the control of independent spending the most important question in campaign finance regulation in the 1990s. Drastic steps such as an outright ban on their activities will probably never pass into law, but more benign-sounding proposals for regulations may succeed. Congress may extend the reporting and administrative rules that apply to corporate PACs to noncorporate PACs. This would impose large fixed costs that many tiny movements cannot afford and would work in the interests of the main parties.

The movement to protect parties and incumbents exists in all industrialized democracies. In his studies of Europe, North America, and Israel, Paltiel drew attention to the remarkably similar efforts by the established parties of all countries to exclude outsiders from participating in politics (1979, 1980, 1981). Canada is the example closest to home. In 1983 the three main parties unanimously banned independent spending in federal elections. The law has never been enforced because of strong questions about whether it violates the constitution, but efforts by incumbents to see it enforced have not eased.[6]

Politicians get support from some scholars who see nothing wrong in a system of strong parties, kept strong by the state. These scholars look on independent spenders as troublesome latecomers to the American political scene.[7] They believe that the main parties ease tensions between groups with different aims. Parties are said to "channel" and "reconcile" conflict in society. Allowing independent groups to compete with one another and with politicians hinders parties in their traditional role and makes it hard to know who speaks for the people. The invariable conclusion is that something must be done to redress the imagined imbalance of resources between parties and outside groups. Larry Sabato, a prominent voice in the campaign finance debate during the 1980s, described independent groups' activities as "noxious" and wrote that "even though independent spending itself should not be restricted, its unfortunate effects can be tempered somewhat [by] strengthening the financial role of parties in elections" (1987, p. 175). This view is common among academics and politicians.

No one can argue that parties do not serve an important function. Voters benefit by selecting a small group of professionals to specialize in representing their interests. Voters also understand that by smoothing differences of opinion major parties can organize large numbers of people into a powerful political force. But these benefits flow only when professional politicians tender their services in competition with all alternatives. The benefits cannot be preserved in law. Parties must earn respect. They must protect themselves by meeting challenges head-on, resisting the urge to declare themselves an endangered species.

## Spending Limits and Campaign Costs

Competition is not the only casualty of spending limits. Limits can actually increase the cost of elections. One of the most common pretexts for limits is that they lower costs by capping what candidates spend. But, as argued in Chapter 2, spending is not a good measure of cost. Cost is what has to be spent to get a result, such as informing a certain number of voters. Ironically, limits may increase costs by forcing candidates to look for ways around limits. In an open society like the United States limits on free speech have little moral appeal. Spending-limit laws will not attract the obedience of a majority of the public. Intelligent, well-meaning people will devote themselves to finding legal ways to frustrate the spirit of the law. This may thwart the anticompetitive effects of limits but valuable human and physical resources will be wasted in the act.

At the federal level only presidential candidates who accept public financing have to keep their spending down. In 1988 public financing came to $46 million for each major party candidate. Candidates who do not abide by the limit pass up this rich subsidy. Since the Federal Election Campaign Act took hold in 1976, the race for the presidency has been a search for ways to get public money while at the same time spending more than is allowed. The clever schemes which candidates use fascinate the press and are worthy of mention for the effort behind them.[8]

There are two types of presidential spending limits: one which applies to primaries and one which applies to the general election. Each limit has loopholes. Before a party nominates its leader, any candidate may raise money and receive matching funds for contributions of $250 or less, up to a limit of roughly 16 cents per eligible voter. (In 1990 this worked out to $10,000,000 in 1974 dollars. (See column 1 of Table 2). During the late 1970s, Ronald Reagan evaded this prenomination limit by using the presidential political action committee (PAC), a device which allowed him to campaign without campaigning. Reagan set up his own PAC to contribute money to conservative candidates at state and local levels. In turn these candidates invited him to speak in their constituencies and paid his travel, hired consultants, raised funds, and recruited volunteers. This allowed him to campaign long before declaring his candidacy for the Republican leadership and falling under the prenomination limit. By 1988, almost every major contender in the presidential primaries had his own PAC—for example, George Bush's Fund for America's Future and Jack Kemp's Campaign for Prosperity.

TABLE 2
Major Party Campaign Expenditure Limits and Public Funding
(in millions of dollars)

| | Prenomination campaign | | | | General election campaign | | |
|---|---|---|---|---|---|---|---|
| | National spending limit[a] | Exempt fundraising[b] | Overall spending limit[c] | Nominating convention | Public treasury grant[d] | National party spending limit[e] | Overall spending limit[f] |
| 1976 | 10.9 | 2.2 | 13.1 | 2.2[g] | 21.8 | 3.2 | 25.0 |
| 1980 | 14.7 | 2.9 | 17.7 | 4.4 | 29.4 | 4.6 | 34.0 |
| 1984 | 20.2 | 4.0 | 24.2 | 8.1 | 40.4 | 6.9 | 47.3 |
| 1988 | 23.1 | 4.6 | 27.7 | 9.2 | 46.1 | 8.3 | 54.4 |
| 1992 | 27.6 | 5.5 | 33.1 | 11.0 | 55.2 | 10.3 | 65.5 |

a. Based on $10 million plus cost-of-living-allowance (COLA) increases, using 1974 as the base year. Eligible candidates may receive no more than one-half the national spending limit in public matching funds. Publicly funded candidates must observe spending limits in the individual states equal to the greater of $200,000 + COLA (with 1974 as the base year) or $0.16 times the voting-age population (VAP) + COLA.
b. Candidates may spend up to 20 percent of the national spending limit for fundraising.
c. Legal and accounting expenses to ensure compliance with the law are exempt from the spending limit.
d. Based on $20 million + COLA.
e. Based on $0.20 times VAP + COLA.
f. Compliance costs are exempt from the spending limit.
g. Based on $2 million + COLA. Under the 1979 FECA amendments, the basic grant was raised to $3 million. In 1984, Congress raised the basic grant to $4 million.
*Sources:* Alexander and Bauer 1991, p. 14, and personal communication from Alexander, 1993.

Presidential PACs are not the only way to avoid limits. In 1984 Vice President Walter Mondale discovered a loophole that allowed delegates to the national convention to spend money on buttons, bumper stickers, and other modest advertisements. Because the delegates were supposed to be independent of the Mondale campaign they could accept and spend PAC money without limit. The FEC investigated and found these committees not to be truly independent (Germond and Witcover 1985). Other ruses abound, such as Gary Hart's use of a think tank through which to spend money on developing issues for his campaign (Riordan 1987).

### Soft Money

To get around postnomination limits both parties spend "soft money." Hard money is the funding a presidential candidate gets from the government and the small amount his party is allowed to spend to promote him directly. Soft money is money raised under *state* laws that is used to influence *federal* elections (Alston 1992). State and local parties can spend on political mailings, on drives to register voters, and on bringing voters to the polls. Federal law has no say over contributions to and spending by state and local parties for this purpose. State laws vary, but thirty states allow corporations to give as much as they wish from their own treasuries to state parties, and forty-one states allow direct labor union contributions (Alexander 1991, p. 24). This in effect bypasses the tight limits on PAC and individual contributions. Officials of presidential campaigns and special private "brokers" raise most of the soft money and both parties have exclusive clubs to which they admit donors of $100,000 or more. Presidential candidates hold receptions for club members and in 1988 this sort of special treatment convinced at least 375 people to join either the Republican or Democratic versions (Magelby and Nelson 1990). The rise in soft-money spending, summarized in Table 3, was one reason behind cries for reform in the early 1990s. These cries convinced President Bill Clinton to announce a plan to ban all soft money from use in federal elections.

These examples suggest that there are ways around limits but do not show that limits have no effect. Parties pay a price for the lawyers they retain to find loopholes. Some of the ploys these lawyers invent call for low-level party members to spend on a candidate's behalf. To direct the lower echelons in this manner, in a national campaign lasting several years, candidates must assign experienced staff and engage consultants, accountants, and dozens of different specialists. Neither specialists nor lawyers do anything productive; they just find ways around the man-made obstacles created by limits.

It is possible to obtain an idea of the cost of collecting soft money by looking at what candidates spend from their "compliance funds." To pay the expense of organizing the soft-money effort candidates draw on what is known as a "compliance fund." Money from the fund is officially supposed to pay the legal and accounting costs of sticking to election laws and FEC regulations. Such expenditures do not count toward the candidate's spending limit and "FEC regulations allow campaigns to use the funds to pick up the tab for at least 10 percent of their headquarters' payroll and overhead" (Montgomery 1989). In practice, any cost attributable to the existence of federal election laws can be counted as a compliance expense. Both major parties have interpreted this broadly to mean that they can use compliance funds to guide the collection and spending of soft

TABLE 3
Soft Money Raised in Presidential Campaigns
(in millions of 1992 dollars)

|      | Democrats | Republicans | Total |
|------|-----------|-------------|-------|
| 1980 | 6.62      | 24.98       | 31.60 |
| 1984 | 7.88      | 20.48       | 28.36 |
| 1988 | 26.48     | 25.33       | 51.81 |
| 1992 | 19.80     | 12.50       | 32.30 |

Sources: 1980–1988 data compiled from Table 3.3 in Alexander and Bauer 1991, p. 37. 1992 data is for the period July 1, 1992, to November 23, 1992, and comes from Common Cause.

money. Party lawyers answer innumerable questions from campaign workers about what the law allows and advise them on how to keep campaign and soft-money operations apart. In 1988 Democrats raised $2.9 million and Republicans $4 million to keep their compliance funds stocked (Montgomery 1989, pp. 30–31). This is an imperfect measure of the cost of compliance but gives us an idea of its order of magnitude, which appears to be in the millions of dollars.

The point to note is that it costs more than a dollar to spend a dollar of soft money. Complying adds to the expense. In addition, soft money may not be as productive as legal campaign tender because candidates cannot use it as they wish. It is true that the money a party spends encouraging voters to register wins public recognition and goodwill, but there may be better ways to run a campaign. The same amount spent directly advertising the candidate's views may be of greater value to the candidate and of more interest to the public.

In 1992 Congress passed limits on how much could be spent on soft-money activities. The House defined these activities as "anything 'in connection' with a federal and non-federal election, including but not limited to slate cards, sample ballots, voter registration, identification and election day turnout drives and fundraisers that benefit federal and state candidates" (Alston 1992, p. 492). President Bush vetoed these limits, but had he not, candidates would no doubt have continued their brilliant but wasteful search for new loopholes.

In 1993 President Clinton proposed a complete ban on soft money in federal elections. Under the plan all state party grassroots activities such as "get out the vote" drives and voter registration would be paid for by hard money. But the federal government would give presidential candidates a subsidy of two cents per voter to support grassroots activity. As I explain in the next chapter, such a subsidy may be as wasteful as a spending limit.

## The Future of Spending Limits

I have argued here that spending limits and campaign subsidies protect incumbents from challenger attacks while sparing them the expense of fighting tiresome election battles.

The potentially self-serving motives behind these legislative proposals are not widely recognized, and campaign spending limits continue to get media attention for the wrong reasons. The use of soft money by both major parties to get around presidential limits has focused the debate on how to eliminate loopholes in campaign law. As a result the most important questions surrounding limits have gone unanswered. Are spending limits incumbent-protection laws? Do they increase the cost of American elections?

---

"Spending limits not only protect incumbents but generate waste. Candidates spend close to 10 percent of their budgets figuring ways around the laws and coordinating their quasi-legal activities."

---

To answer, we need to understand how spending works in elections and how it influences political competition. I have argued that it helps to think of competition as a state in which candidates or single-issue groups may contest one another's records and ideas freely. Money can give a candidate an unfair advantage if he is the only one allowed to spend it. Incumbents can come close to doing this by spending government money to promote themselves while in office and limiting what everyone can spend during the election campaign. Incumbents who cannot protect themselves with a spending limit cannot bank on the goodwill they generate with government funds while in office and must be ready to merge their opponents' platforms into their own. They may survive for many years like this, but as the public's servants, not as a protected, privileged caste.

Spending limits not only protect incumbents but generate waste. Candidates spend close to 10 percent of their budgets figuring ways around the laws and coordinating their quasi-legal activities. These activities win candidates some support but are not very good at informing voters of the issues. This is a less visible but no less serious cost of limiting spending.

Future incumbent-led reforms may concentrate on limiting what independent groups and individuals can spend to promote or oppose candidates. As information and communication technology advances independents will pose an ever more formidable challenge to the established parties. The potential power of independents may have been behind three initiatives in the 1980s by Democratic members of Congress to amend the Constitution and clear the way for limits on forms of spending. The positive role of independents should be recognized and their activities should not be hindered by limits or by subsidies to the major parties.

# 5

# *Political Foodstamps for Candidates*

The moment governments get into a position to control the purse-strings of their political opponents is also the moment at which dissent in any society makes an unconditional surrender to conformity.

Anthony Howard, *political commentator*

CAMPAIGN SUBSIDIES SEEM LIKE A sensible way to keep politicians safe from the influence of special interests. Public money with no strings attached is supposed to replace private, potentially corrupting contributions and is seen as the "essential element for making political money fully accountable to voters" (Adamany 1990, p. 111). Subsidies are also seen as a way of promoting competition between candidates. These views are popular among reformers even though there is little evidence to support them. Influence peddling and corruption occur in countries where the state funds elections. There are many ways to sway politicians; if special interests cannot use contributions during the election to get what they want they can always spend more time lobbying the winners after the election. What evidence we have on the effect of subsidies suggests that established parties use them to keep new movements down. Canada, Britain, Italy, and

*this is to be expected in a rts/pret orientedregime, b/c the preferences/citizens are pro-form*

75

Germany give money on the basis of past electoral performance, building inertia into elections and protecting large parties.

Even though the U.S. government gives away over $100 million to presidential hopefuls every four years, surprisingly few hard questions about the wisdom of this expensive policy have been asked. The critical question, "Do subsidies encourage the selection of candidates of high quality?" still awaits an answer. The most popular criticism of subsidies is that candidates who are not popular enough to get money from the public should not get money from the state. It is less widely mentioned that subsidies may actually lessen what voters know about their candidates and lead to bad political choices. Subsidies give candidates of uncertain quality a boost by reducing their dependence on the public's approval and contributions. The number of contributions received by a candidate is an expression of public opinion. Subsidies obscure this vital cue and help candidates who were never popular to begin with or candidates who have fallen out of favor to sustain themselves in a campaign.

If there is a role for subsidies, it should be to give voters information for which they have a demand. This would mean subsidizing not only candidates but also issue groups, labor unions, and corporations. It is not practical to choose which groups deserve money, but the difficulty of deciding how much to give candidates is no less real. In economic policy government has shown itself inept at picking which industries should be promoted, and there is no reason to believe that politics is any different. The present system gives more than $50 million to each of the two major parties and a much smaller sum on a sliding scale to minor parties. Independent candidates get almost no help. The law rigidly doles out money to parties which may have lost their popular support and makes it difficult for outsiders to contest the presidency. The law also shows little ability to support ideas for which there is new demand and actively stifles ideas and movements that have just started to grow.

This chapter describes the present system of presidential subsidies and recent efforts to extend them to members of Congress. I review the formal reasons for and against subsidies and analyze the Supreme Court's decision to uphold presidential subsidies in its 1976 *Buckley v. Valeo* ruling.

## The Federal System of Campaign Subsidies

At the federal level only presidential hopefuls may ask for money. The subsidies are part of the Revenue Act of 1971, which was signed into law by President Richard Nixon. They are paid from a Presidential Election Campaign Fund nourished by taxpayers, who once a year may designate a dollar of their liability to the fund. This designation is referred to as a tax checkoff.[1] The 1971 Revenue Act also gave tax credits and tax deductions for political contributions. The deductions were raised from $50 to $100 in the 1974 amendments to the Federal Election Campaign Act (FECA), but were repealed altogether by the Revenue Act of 1978. To compensate, the Revenue Act of 1978 raised the tax credit to $50, but the reform of the tax system in 1986 got rid of the tax credit. Congress has tried since the early 1970s to vote itself subsidies, without success. In 1992 Democrats led an initiative in both the Senate and the House to pass subsidies for Congress members. President George Bush immediately vetoed the move. Since 1976, when the first presidential subsidies were granted, the federal government has paid candidates $650 million (in equivalent 1991 dollars). Table 4 summarizes these grants and compares them to private contributions to presidential races.

### How the Law Works Today

A candidate who accepts money from the Presidential Election Campaign Fund must stick to an official spending ceiling. In theory, anyone running for office may qualify, but the size of the subsidy depends on whether one is a "major," "minor," or "new" party candidate. A major party is a party whose candidate for president in the most recent election got at least 25 percent of the popular vote (U.S.C. 9002[6]). A minor party is a party whose candidate got between 5 percent and 25 percent of the vote. All other parties are "new" (U.S.C. 9002[8]). Candidates who do not run under a party banner are referred to as independent candidates.

The fund gives money for primaries, party nominating conventions, and the general election campaign. To get money for primaries a candidate must establish credibility by collecting private contributions of $5,000 in each of twenty states in amounts

TABLE 4
Private and Public Funding of Presidential Primary and General Election Campaigns, 1976–1988 (in millions of 1992 dollars)

| | Private funds | | |
| | Primary | General election | |
| --- | --- | --- | --- |
| 1976 | 108.3 | | |
| 1980 | 104.6 | | |
| 1984 | 85.5 | | |
| 1988 | 168.4 | | |

| | U.S. Treasury funds | | |
| | Primary | General election | Primary + general election |
| --- | --- | --- | --- |
| 1976 | 60.4 | 108.3 | 168.7 |
| 1980 | 53.0 | 107.5 | 160.5 |
| 1984 | 47.5 | 109.3 | 156.8 |
| 1988 | 78.4 | 110.0 | 188.4 |
| 1992 | — | 110.5 | — |

Note: Blank cell = not applicable. Dash = not available. To be eligible to receive matching funds a candidate must first raise $100,000 in contributions from individuals. At least $5,000 must come from each of twenty different states in amounts of no more than $250 from any individual contributor.
Sources: FEC press release, March 29, 1993; U.S. Department of Commerce. Statistical Abstract of the United States, 1991, 1980; U.S. Department of Commerce. Survey of Current Business, March 1993.

no greater than $250 (U.S.C. 9033[b]). This entitles him or her to a federal matching grant for every contribution of $250 or less. Candidates who accept money from the fund may not spend more than $50,000 of their personal funds on election. The limit on spending in primaries is roughly half the limit for the general election campaign, and subsidies to a primary candidate cannot come to more than half of the primary spending limit. This means that candidates who accept subsidies can spend up to $10 million (in 1974 dollars) in their primaries and receive up to $5 million from the fund (in 1974 dollars).[2] Minor party and new party candidates are eligible.

Major parties each get $4 million (in 1974 dollars) to hold their nominating conventions (U.S.C. 9008[b][1]). A minor party gets a fraction of this based on how well its candidate did relative to the major parties in the last election.[3] New party candidates get nothing.

Major party candidates get $20 million from the fund (in 1974 dollars) to run their general election campaigns and may not receive private contributions or spend more than $50,000 of their own money. Minor parties get a fraction of $20 million based on how well they did in the last election relative to the major parties.[4] New candidates can get money *after* the election, provided they win at least 5 percent of the popular vote. Their postelection reimbursement depends on how well they did at the polls. New party candidates who do not meet the 5 percent threshold are not reimbursed. Independent candidates cannot receive federal subsidies of any sort, for any purpose.

## Subsidies and Outsiders

The most direct criticism of the U.S. system of subsidies is that the system is not kind to dark-horse candidates in the major parties or to outsiders such as independent candidates. Matching grants in primaries go disproportionately to candidates with the most funding. This builds inertia into what should be the most dynamic stage in the race for the presidency. New parties get no money to run their nominating conventions, and independent candidates receive no money at all. These rules of the game cannot exclude independents and new parties with extraordinary popular appeal, but they may keep minor political movements from contesting the major parties as effectively as they could without subsidies.

Parties have been forced to defend these rules on the ground that giving money to outsiders promotes frivolity and factionalism. In *Buckley* the Supreme Court also took this stance, explaining that "Congress' interest is not in funding hopeless candidacies with large sums of public money. . . . An eligibility requirement for public funds . . . serves the important public interest against providing artificial incentives to 'splintered parties and unrestrained factionalism'" (424 U.S. 1 [1976], p. 671). The message is that outsiders contribute little to politics and do not deserve support. The trend in federal politics over the past fifteen years suggests that, contrary to the established parties' wish to claim the main role, voters are looking more to issue groups for information and to independent candidates for their leaders. The presidential subsidies were passed at a time of great stability in politics. With the exception of Teddy Roosevelt in 1912, no independent had outpolled a major party candidate since 1856.

In giving its blessing to presidential subsidies, the Supreme Court did not take into account that information technology was changing in favor of outsiders and that soon Americans would want to hear more of what these groups had to say.

If demand grows for new parties, the 5 percent threshold for funding will tilt the field even more sharply in favor of the old, established parties. If three new parties appear, for example, and each obtains a little less than 5 percent of the popular vote, nearly 15 percent of the electorate will get no government money to support their positions. None of these groups can win, but that is seldom the purpose of fringe parties. They exist to get their ideas across by putting pressure on the big parties. Public money will give an artificial boost to established parties or any party that gets more than 5 percent of the vote.

New parties that win more than 5 percent of the vote get government money after the election, but this subsidy is not as helpful as it seems. Candidates can use the expected reimbursement to secure campaign loans from banks or private creditors, but the problem is that under election law loans other than those from banks are considered to be contributions until they are repaid (U.S.C. 431[8][A][i]).[5] Limits that apply to contributions also apply to loans, which means that a new party can only bank against its anticipated performance by borrowing $1,000 sums (the limit on individual contributions to candidates) from many different sources. Finding these loans and reporting them to the FEC eats up the independent candidate's time and money. Major and minor parties do not pay these costs because they get their money up-front, before the election.

Up-front grants are another example of why presidential subsidies may be too rigid to reflect voter demand. In *Buckley v. Valeo* the Supreme Court denied that giving the major parties a flat grant up-front enhanced their ability to campaign, arguing that "it [the subsidy law] substitutes public funding for what the parties would raise privately and additionally imposes an expenditure limit" (p. 671). The unstated assumption was that the major parties would always be able to raise money up to their limits. In the future this may no longer be the case, and major parties on their way to becoming minor parties will find that the flat grant slows their decline.

By giving too much money to the big parties, subsidy laws make it harder for small parties to raise money. As I argue in Chapter 7, contributions depend in part on one's chances of winning. Anything that lowers a party's chances lowers its contributions, which in turn lowers its chances, and so on. In *Buckley v. Valeo* the Supreme Court argued that "new parties will be unfinanced . . . only if they are unable to get private financial support, which presumably reflects a general lack of support for the party. Public financing of some candidates does not make private fundraising for others any more difficult" (p. 671). This position is only true if public financing does not change any party's chances of winning. Perhaps the strangest effect of presidential subsidies is that they may encourage the wealthy to run in elections. By making it hard to borrow money against future reimbursements, the law leaves room only for extremely popular independent candidates who can count on an avalanche of contributions and wealthy independent candidates who can finance their own campaigns. The problem is due to the contribution law which keeps a candidate from accepting more than $1,000 in loans from private sources. As House Representative Dick Cheney explained, "the limitation on contributions has placed a higher premium than ever before on candidates who are able and willing to invest their personal wealth in a race" (1980, p. 245).

Similar conditions which make it hard for minor candidates to run in presidential elections appear in a recent proposal by President Bill Clinton for subsidies to members of Congress. The proposal is an example of how thresholds for qualification can favor incumbents. In the president's plan both Senate and House candidates can submit to "voluntary spending limits" ($600,000 for House candidates and ranging from $1.2 million to $5.5 million for Senate candidates) in return for public campaign subsidies. But only Senate candidates who can raise 10 percent of the general election spending limit in individual contributions of $250 or less can apply for the subsidies. These subsidies take the form of vouchers which candidates can spend on communications. The value of these vouchers would be 12.5 percent of the candidate's spending limit. In the House, candidates must raise 15 percent of the spending limit ($90,000) in individual contributions of $200 or less, in order to qualify for communications vouchers made available on a matching-funds basis up to $200,000. Incumbents meet these thresholds more easily than challengers and outsiders, because they already have a fund-raising organization in place.

### "The Freedom Not to Grovel"

In summary, the measure of harm caused by subsidies depends on the weight one attaches to election outcomes. The present system of subsidies probably has little effect on who wins and loses. But subsidies can reduce the amount of pressure outsiders put on established parties. The *New York Times* praised this result, declaring that "public financing confers on presidential candidates the freedom not to grovel," and the *Washington Post* noted that subsidies have freed the candidates from having to "tin-cup it around the country" (Wertheimer 1991, p. 44). In an article for the *New York Times Magazine* (March 14, 1993), political analyst Elizabeth Drew suggested that members of Congress could find a relief in subsidies similar to that experienced by their presidential counterparts. She argued that fundraising warps a senator's life, beginning the day after the election is won and never stopping. Senators, who must spend $4 million on average to run a competitive race, are forced to raise $12,500 a week and many of them find such "panhandling" demeaning.

Herbert Alexander, perhaps the foremost expert on election finance law, warns against the excessive sympathy for politicians that Drew and Wertheimer show and questions the need for electoral welfare payments: "By protecting parties from the failure which results from a lack of public enthusiasm for their plat-forms, public financing may make it less necessary for parties to respond to the real political issues of the day, thereby interfering with the effectiveness and responsiveness of the political system as a whole" (1989, p. 16). Academics who agree on this point can be found from the left to the right on the political spectrum. As the neo-Marxist political scientist Leo Panitch wrote, "Although the foray by the state into the regulation of party financing . . . ostensibly seeks to limit the influence of corporate money . . . the introduction of state financing as a substitute, carrying as it does a bias in favor of existing parties, may tend to freeze the extremely limited alternatives presently available" (Panitch 1977, p. 10).

In the years since the presidential subsidy law passed, minor parties and candidates have been almost absent from elections. The problem may be more grave in the future, because the trend for the 1990s indicates that voters will give more of their attention to outsiders and will on occasion chasten the major parties by relegating them to a minority. The rise of independent Ross Perot in the 1992 campaign is an example of what may occur.

## What Are Subsidies Worth to Voters?

Subsidies may favor insiders over outsiders, but there is little evidence that they have given one of the major parties an edge over the other. In 1971 Democrats imposed presidential contribution and spending limits to end the Republican fundraising advantage and voted for subsidies to take the strain out of running for office. But subsequent amendments to the Federal Election Campaign Act left loopholes which allowed presidential candidates to spend as much as they wished. Since both parties get the same federal assistance and in practice raise as much money as they can obtain from private contributors, neither is any further ahead.

---

"Subsidies are a costly way of getting information across because they diminish the role of the contributor and in so doing remove a guide to where the candidates stand and what the issues are."

---

Because subsidies have become a supplement to contributions instead of a substitute as the law intended, voters may be more informed about the major parties and can make more intelligent choices between the two. Whether this makes the subsidy worthwhile is impossible to say. Those who believe that power should be shared only between the major parties might answer in the affirmative. Those who believe independent movements can force the major parties to be innovative and responsive might disagree. The only general statement that can be made is that a dollar in subsidies does not give voters as much information as a dollar in private contributions.

Subsidies do not reflect how much support a party has. At best they reflect the fact that a party is major or minor. On the other hand, voters may use the size of contributions to gauge how popular a party is, and this information can be used to decide which party to vote for. This means that the subsidized part of the race is less informative than the part funded by private contributors. Subsidies are a costly way of getting information across because they diminish the role of the contributor and in so doing remove a guide to where the candidates stand and what the issues are.

## Congressional Subsidies

Unlike the presidency, Congress has never had subsidies. Some students of campaign reform, and most of the Democrats who sit in Congress, believe the situation should be changed. They base their argument on the common finding that money benefits congressional challengers more than incumbents (see Chapter 4 on limits). Could not an equal subsidy to all candidates improve the position of challengers and increase competition? Would this not be a welcome way of lowering the high reelection rate of incumbent members of Congress?

The answer depends on one's interpretation of high reelection rates and of the greater power of challenger spending. As explained in Chapter 4, high turnover should not be the direct goal of policy. What is important is that challengers be able to contest incumbents by soliciting the support of their contributors. If the money a challenger spends reflects not the support of contributors but an automatic subsidy, it may send the wrong message to voters.

Many challengers who have come close to winning say that a few thousand more dollars would have taken them over the top. If one looks at how productive their small campaign funds are, this argument is hard to dispute. But productivity of funds is only half the picture. This is because productivity, as measured by the statistical studies cited in Chapter 4 (Abramowitz 1988, Jacobson 1978, 1985), gives only a "local" idea of the candidate's strength. Even untalented, unappealing candidates may get excellent mileage from the first few thousand dollars they spend. Once they have won over the small number of voters who are willing to support them, the remainder of their spending may not get them much further. It is not clear how much more competitive elections would be if challengers got subsidies; it is not even clear that the majority of voters would be served by such artificial promotion.

Figure 7 illustrates the point that even though challenger spending may get more votes than incumbent spending, subsidies are not guaranteed to promote competition. The incumbent vote curve shows how many votes a hypothetical incumbent can expect for any amount he spends, holding all else constant. The challenger vote curve does the same for the challenger. The

FIGURE 7
Why Subsidies May Not Make Challengers As Well Off As Is Believed

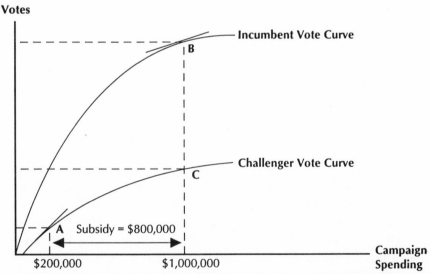

Note: Slope at A > slope at B. Campaign spending has a diminishing effect on a candidate's votes. More spending (all else remaining constant) increases votes, but at a falling rate. Initially the challenger is at point A and the incumbent at point B. At point A every extra dollar the challenger spends brings in more votes than the incumbent receives at point B. This does not mean, however, that the challenger would win if a subsidy was received which allowed him or her to spend as much as the incumbent does. With such a subsidy the challenger ends up at point C, still obtaining fewer votes than the incumbent.
Source: Author.

steepness of a curve at any point shows how many new votes the candidate gets by spending an additional dollar. The curves get less steep as spending rises, which indicates that an additional dollar brings in fewer votes than the previous dollar; there are diminishing returns to spending. In this example the incumbent spends five dollars for each of the challenger's dollars. The steepness of the challenger's curve at point A indicates that if he were to spend an extra dollar he would get an extra two votes. At point B, the incumbent gets only one vote per dollar. But this does not mean that a subsidy to the challenger, closing the gap in spending between the two candidates, would make the challenger win. Even if both spend the same amount (point C), the incumbent still wins.[6]

There is no mystery in this result. The challenger gets a higher return for his extra dollar because he has not yet saturated the market with advertising. This does not mean that he would win if all resources were equalized. In Figure 7 the incumbent's vote curve lies above the challenger's, reflecting that he is a more appealing and skilful candidate. Given equal resources the incumbent still wins.

---

"In politics, grants may advance the fortunes of a candidate at the expense of voter-taxpayers who prefer a different candidate."

---

The subsidy increases the challenger's vote, and this may put pressure on the incumbent to pay attention to some of the issues raised by the challenger. Is this not a desirable effect? Here a comparison with industrial strategy helps to sharpen the picture. Government grants can allow a small, "underfunded" industry to survive and maybe even thrive. But the money is taken from taxpayers who show by their voluntary savings and investment decisions that they would prefer to put their money in other industries. In politics, grants may advance the fortunes of a candidate at the expense of voter-taxpayers who prefer a different candidate.

Of course politics is not only about choosing which interest group will dominate but also about finding someone who will manage government efficiently in the interests of all voters. Just as industrial strategy grants interfere with the market's selection of the fittest producers, political grants may not promote the best people to office. Subsidies weaken the link between the informed judgment of contributors and the resources candidates use to promote themselves. Subsidies may allow challengers to better challenge incumbents, but this does not reflect the support challengers would get if they were left to their own devices. A policy of simply *allowing,* and not subsidizing, challengers to contest incumbents will produce an electoral system in which outcomes more closely reflect the quality of the candidates.

### Prospects for Congressional Reform

Republicans oppose public funding mainly because it is tied to spending limits. Even though their advantage has diminished in recent years, they still raise more money than Democrats. The bills which Democratic senator David Boren championed in the 1980s and 1990s (S2 and S3) would have reduced what Republicans could spend while supplying Democrats with enough money to bring them onto the same level as their opponents. Republicans such as Senator Bob Packwood see these bills as attempts by Democrats "to take three or four hundred million dollars from taxpayers . . . to perpetuate their majority in the U.S. Congress" (Alexander and Bauer 1991, p. 112).

If the major parties ever agree it will be at a time when neither has an edge in fundraising. The law that passes will probably work strongly in favor of the established parties and against outside candidates and groups. Senate Resolution 3, which President Bush vetoed in 1992, may be a precursor of such a law. Had it not been for the spending-limit provisions, S3 might have passed. Candidates of both established parties would have received matching grants for every dollar above $10,000 that independent groups spent to oppose them. It is not hard to see who would have benefited from such a rule.

## Subsidies Tilt the Field

Election subsidies are supposed to keep candidates from being "bought out" by special interests, but instead they may entrench the established parties and make it hard for outsiders to compete.

The intellectual defense of subsidies is that they are needed to right an imbalance in campaign funding which occurs because contributors give "too much" money to incumbents and "too little" to challengers. This is said to concentrate power in a few hands and to make the public cynical about politicians.

This chapter has taken a different view. Political subsidies are money taken from one group in society and given to another group which is not popular enough to raise the money itself. They do not stop corruption, nor do they encourage public confidence. As Winter writes, "We ought to ask . . . whether confidence is likely to be restored when taxpayers pay for campaigns they regard as frivolous, wasteful, and, in some cases, abhorrent. Would the taxpayer viewing television spots have more confidence because part of the tab came out of his paycheck? Would the voter have more confidence because he had to help pay for activities with which he disagreed?" (1973).

Because there is little evidence that campaign money buys candidates, it is hard to find a public interest reason for subsidies. The specific interest is easier to see. The established parties have passed presidential subsidies which favor candidates with the most public support. Matching grants in primaries may give candidates who are already popular an added edge over their challengers. The biases built into subsidies continue after the primaries. During the general election big parties can get around their spending limits by raising soft money. This makes their subsidies of more than $50 million complements to their privately stocked war chests. In contrast, outsiders cannot qualify for subsidies until *after* the election and must reach a 5 percent threshold of the national vote before they are reimbursed. Congress receives no subsidies but has tried repeatedly throughout the 1980s and in the early 1990s to pass laws that would favor the incumbent Democratic party over the challenging Republicans. Alexander summarizes neatly the principle at work in all these cases: "Public funding can add to the power of government if the party in power gains control over the funding of its opposition. The advantages of incumbency extend to the formulas used to define who gets public funding and under what conditions" (1989, p. 18).

The lack of a fair subsidy may not be the reason that challengers fail to win office. This, however, is not the point when considering the damage such a subsidy may do. Successful incumbents are the ones who take heed of the issues raised by popular challengers and adapt to public demands. Subsidies that tilt the field against challengers and outside pressure groups may make it easier for incumbents to be less attentive.

# 6

# *The Myth of Contributions and Corruption*

Contributions . . . serve as a barometer of the intensity of
voter feeling. In a majoritarian system voters who feel exceptionally
strongly about particular issues may be unable to reflect their
feelings adequately in periodic votes. As members of the
antiwar movement often pointed out, the strength of their
feelings as well as their numbers should be taken into
account. . . . Campaign contributions are perhaps the most
important means by which such intensity can be expressed.

Ralph K. Winter, *legal scholar*

JOURNALISTS AND PUBLIC INTEREST GROUPS such as Common Cause
rightly view the most important section of the Federal Election
Campaign Act (FECA) as a failure, but they reach this view for
the wrong reasons. The FECA, which was forged in the 1970s,
limited what individuals and groups could give to candidates
and encouraged them to give through tightly regulated "political
action committees" (PACs). Large donors soon discovered they
could set up many PACs and give as much as they did before.
This started a chorus for even tighter regulation, which peaked
when President Bush declared in 1989 that he would like to do
away with PACs altogether. The policy debate has turned in circles
for twenty years in a search for more effective laws. The main
criticism of the present law is that it does not go far enough

and that a definitive contribution law must be drafted in order to end the open spectacle of special interests carving up Washington.

In this chapter I argue that contribution-limit laws are a failure for wholly different reasons. Based on the shaky principle that campaign money corrupts government, these laws actually serve to discourage voters from expressing the intensity of their preferences, reduce the information voters receive, and increase the costs of political campaigns.

Contributions excite passion because they are visible. Why do PACs give most of their money to incumbents? Why do they sometimes give to *both* candidates in a race? Two decades of exhaustive academic research has found no conclusive evidence that election money buys government favors.[1] The high visibility of contributions has made this area of study popular, which has unfortunately left a gap in what we know about other types of interest group activity such as lobbying. A guesstimate is that interest groups devote perhaps only 10 percent of their resources to contributing. This suggests that public concerns about the importance of contributions may be out of proportion to their influence on government decision making. Contributions are not a sideshow, but neither do they make up the entire picture of how public policy is influenced. Eliminating or limiting contributions will not stop the pressures that are put on politicians but will direct these pressures through other channels.

Because motivation, talent, and wealth are not distributed evenly across the population, some groups are bound to have a natural advantage in influencing government. Farmers form less than 6 percent of the population but have remarkable sway over legislators. Their common outlook and economic interests help them to work together. They face little opposition because the cost of supporting them is thinly spread over too many consumers with too little in common. No reasonable restriction on contributions will even out the natural political advantages of all groups. Forbidding contributions from farmers might result in lower food prices for consumers, but such a policy would not be reasonable because a thousand similar examples exist. A growth in the wealth of politically talented groups must be accepted as a feature of any society in which the government controls close to half of the gross national product. Government has proved inept at distributing these resources with efficient results, but the answer to this problem should not be sought through the regulation of contributions.

## Contribution Law

Federal contribution law is a confusing mishmash of limits, exceptions to the rules, and jargon. Table 5, put together by the Federal Election Commission, is a summary of who may contribute how much to whom. A brief history will give some perspective.

Contribution limits are not new to American politics. In 1907 Congress passed the Tilman Act prohibiting chartered banks and corporations from making contributions during elections. This prohibition was extended to labor unions in the 1943 War Labor Disputes Act and the 1947 Labor Management Relations Act. In 1940 amendments to the Hatch Act forbade individuals from giving more than $5,000 to a candidate or political committee. Candidates got around the law by setting up many committees, each ready to accept $5,000 from a large contributor.

Congress prepared for serious reforms throughout the 1960s and took the first step with the 1971 Federal Election Campaign

TABLE 5
Contribution Limits in 1990 (in dollars)

| Source of contribution | To candidate or authorized committee (per election) | To national party committee (per calendar year) | To any other committee (per calendar year) | Total contributions (per calendar year) |
|---|---|---|---|---|
| Individual | 1,000 | 20,000 | 5,000 | 25,000 |
| Multicandidate committee | 5,000 | 15,000 | 5,000 | No limit |
| Party committee | 1,000 or 5,000 | No Limit | 5,000 | No limit |
| Republican or Democratic senatorial campaign committee, or the national party committee, or a combination of both | 17,500 | | | |
| Any other committee or group | 1,000 | 20,000 | 5,000 | No limit |

Blank cell = not applicable.
*Source:* Federal Election Commission.

Act (FECA), which installed the Federal Election Commission and forced candidates to report their spending and contributions. The limits on contributions presented in Table 5 were part of the 1974 amendments to FECA. Big contributions by individuals were eliminated, but FECA opened a new avenue for corporations and labor unions. As before, they were not to contribute from treasury funds, which means profits, operating revenue, and union dues. But now they could use treasury funds to solicit employees, stockholders, or union members for contributions to be placed in a "segregated fund." Segregated funds are known popularly as corporate or labor PACs and are also called "connected" funds. Nonconnected PACs are not affiliated with any business or union and need not set up a segregated fund. They are often referred to as "ideological PACs." Different limits apply to different types of PACs. A PAC with more than fifty contributors which has been registered for more than six months and has made contributions to more than five candidates may give $5,000 to any candidate. PACs in this category are known as multicandidate committees. PACs that do not meet this standard may give only $1,000 per election. Democratic and Republican senatorial committees and the national committees of any party may contribute up to $17,500 to any Senate candidate.

The rules governing PACs did little more than codify a long-standing practice. PACs had been around since the 1930s, when John L. Lewis established labor's Non-Partisan Political League. In 1955 the American Federation of Labor and the Congress of Industrial Organizations merged as the AFL-CIO and formed COPE (Committee on Political Education), which became the model for many PACs (Epstein 1980, p. 110). In the 1960s the Business-Industry PAC (BIPAC) set up a segregated fund, never gave more than $5,000 to any candidate, and submitted to outside audit, in almost perfect anticipation of the future law (Budde 1980, p. 10). It was also a model for other PACs. Labor made the most use of PACs while business found it more efficient to let a few wealthy individuals give large sums on its behalf. General Motors heir Stuart Mott and insurance millionaire Clement Stone are the best known examples of corporate "fat cats" who gave millions of their private fortunes to presidential and congressional candidates.

Labor lobbied hard for the 1974 FECA amendments, in order to clarify the legal status of its committees and protect them from court challenges. It is less certain, but possible, that labor saw a chance in the amendments to hamstring business by outlawing large individual donations. Business, however, soon learned the rules and in the late 1970s overtook labor in creating the greatest number of PACs.

## Trends in Contributions

The drive to restrict contributions has continued since 1974 and is based in part on what appears to be an alarming rise in the number of PACs and the amount of money they give. The crucial question is whether this rise shows that politicians are under greater influence from campaign contributions than before. Conventional wisdom holds that this is obvious, but in fact there is little evidence that politicians are "selling out" more to contributors. The misconceptions about the role of contributions in politics come from a lack of proper attention to the many channels through which people can influence government. This has led reformers to infer too much from the rising trend in contributions.

Most students of politics would agree that as government grows, interest groups will try harder to influence policy. Groups will be especially encouraged if the rules on how to cut the pie are vague or flexible. They will try to influence policy by the most efficient routes, and over time these routes may change. Government wealth is a jackpot for which different groups struggle. A group's outlay should be in proportion to the return it expects. It will divide this outlay on campaigns, lobbying elected officials and bureaucrats, and buying publicity to make its case public and refute other interest group claims.

It can be very misleading to focus simply on contributions. If the government jackpot rises, groups may spend more on all their activities and campaign spending as a fraction of government spending will show up as a constant. But in theory it is also possible that spending on one activity will rise even if government spending falls. A smaller jackpot means that groups will spend less overall; although if one activity becomes very cheap, spending on it may rise. When, for example, mass mailing technology improves and it becomes easier to influence policy by advertising, groups cut back on all other activities and advertise more. Interest groups cannot get as much from government as before because the jackpot is smaller, but one highly visible aspect of their operations—advertising—rises. One should not jump to the conclusion that politicians are "selling out" more.

---

"The misconceptions about the role of contributions in politics come from a lack of proper attention to the many channels through which people can influence government."

---

We can get some feel for the relative importance of contributions by looking at how they have risen as a fraction of government spending. Table 6 and Figure 8 show the sum of contributions to congressional races in election years as a fraction of government spending. Contributions have hovered with no clear trend in the 1980s at around .004 percent of government spending. Contributions have risen in real terms, but so has government spending, and the two have kept rough pace with each other. These numbers are open to many interpretations but are more informative than straight campaign contribution figures. If we assume that outlays to influence government are proportional to the growing government jackpot, then these numbers suggest that contributions today are no more important as a way of gaining influence, relative to other ways, than they were ten years ago.

In sum, there is some evidence that campaign contributions are not rising out of control but are simply keeping pace with the growth of government. Contributions and spending by independent groups have become the center of attention because they are visible, a result of the reporting requirements written in the 1971 FECA. As Sorauf explains, ". . . the 'law of available data' has led to a flowering of research on them [PACs], both by the scholarly community and by journalists and public-interest organizations"

TABLE 6
Election Receipts in All Congressional Campaigns as a Fraction of Government Spending, 1976–1992

| | Congressional receipts (in thousands of dollars) | Federal government spending (in billions of dollars) | Congressional receipts divided by government spending |
|---|---|---|---|
| 1976 | 104,100 | 371.8 | 0.00028 |
| 1978 | 199,400 | 458.7 | 0.00043 |
| 1980 | 248,800 | 590.9 | 0.00042 |
| 1982 | 354,700 | 745.7 | 0.00048 |
| 1984 | 397,200 | 851.8 | 0.00047 |
| 1986 | 472,000 | 990.6 | 0.00048 |
| 1988 | 477,600 | 1,055.9 | 0.00045 |
| 1990 | 471,700 | 1,332.7 | 0.00035 |
| 1992 | 659,000 | 1,458.4 | 0.00045 |

Sources: FEC press releases; U.S. Department of Commerce. *Statistical Abstract of the United States,* 1992, 1989, 1981 editions; U.S. Department of Commerce. *Survey of Current Business,* March 1993.

FIGURE 8
Congressional Campaign Receipts as a Fraction of Federal Government Spending, 1976–1992 (in 1992 dollars)

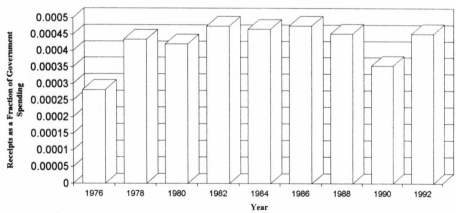

Sources: FEC press release, March 4, 1993; U.S. Department of Commerce. *Statistical Abstract of the United States,* 1992, 1986, 1981 editions; U.S. Department of Commerce. *Survey of Current Business,* March 1993.

(1992, p. 64). If groups had to report what they spent lobbying, a very different debate would be aired in the press and the topic of contributions would be cast in a more meaningful light.

## Contributions: Demand and Supply

The effect of a limit on contributions depends on why candidates take money and why people give it, that is, on demand and supply. On the demand side, candidates seek contributions not only to get elected but to get an idea of how deeply certain constituents feel about certain policies. A limit on contributions reduces this flow of information. On the supply side, people give money in order to influence policy and out of a sense of political duty. Some groups are very good at using contributions to influence outcomes; others excel at lobbying. A limit does not affect all groups equally but holds some back and gives others a leg up.

### Demand

Since candidates are not all alike, they will have many different reasons for accepting money. But there are certain incentives that all candidates face. The effort any candidate puts into winning depends on how powerful and prestigious the office is. As the power and prestige rise, candidates' demand for contributions increases. Candidates for president spend more than congressional candidates because the office is more important and hence there is more competition for it. There are, of course, exceptions. As a matter of principle longtime senator William Proxmire spent little on his successful campaigns.

Even though contributions are vital to the candidate, they probably play little role in subsequent legislative decisions. Contributions do not, with rare exceptions such as certain FBI entrapments of members of Congress in the early 1980s, buy a candidate. Instead they give interest groups "access."[2] Access has a negative connotation and is seen by many as proof that money can open all doors. What critics do not mention is that politicians need some way of knowing how intensely various groups feel about issues. As legal scholar Ralph Winter wrote in a pioneering essay, "This function [of contributions] might be discounted if large contributions reflected only intense but idiosyncratic views. For the most part, however, intense feelings will not gener-ate substantial funds unless large numbers without great wealth also share those convictions. Campaign contributors in these circumstances serve as representatives or surrogates for the entire group" (1973).

A contribution forces a group to commit money to its cause and saves politicians the trouble of weeding out fanciful constituent concerns from serious ones. Contributions establish one's seriousness. They give an interest group an introduction to the candidate, but the group must then make a convincing, informed case that action needs to be taken.

Well-organized interest groups are not the only constituency to which politicians must pay heed. Individuals are an important source of contributions and together give more money to candidates than all PACs combined (see Table 7 and Figure 9). The press and reform advocates seldom emphasize the importance of individual contributions, and the impression most of us are left with is that PAC money dominates politics. This is simply not the case.[3] To tap individual contributions politicians must pay attention to what their individual constituents want and not simply to the demands of special interest groups.

TABLE 7
Funding Sources for Congressional Candidates, 1986–1992

| | Net receipts (in thousands of 1992 dollars) | % from individuals | % from PACs | % from other candidates | % from loans |
|---|---|---|---|---|---|
| **Senate** | | | | | |
| 1986 | 270,236 | 65.3 | 21.1 | 0.9 | 6.1 |
| 1988 | 232,145 | 64.2 | 23.2 | 3.4 | 4.1 |
| 1990 | 196,954 | 64.2 | 22.1 | 1.3 | 5.4 |
| 1992 | 261,620 | 62.1 | 19.8 | 2.5 | 10.8 |
| **House** | | | | | |
| 1986 | 324,215 | 49.5 | 33.9 | 1.8 | 8.1 |
| 1988 | 322,388 | 46.6 | 37.1 | 1.9 | 8.2 |
| 1990 | 300,612 | 45.5 | 38.1 | 1.6 | 7.3 |
| 1992 | 391,680 | 48.6 | 32.8 | 2.9 | 10.7 |

Note: Rows do not add to 100 percent because not all sources of funding are listed. For example, interest on funds in campaign war chests is not included.
Sources: FEC press release, March 4, 1993; U.S. Department of Commerce. Statistical Abstract of the United States, 1992; U.S. Department of Commerce. Survey of Current Business, March 1993.

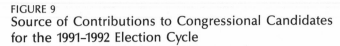

FIGURE 9
Source of Contributions to Congressional Candidates
for the 1991–1992 Election Cycle

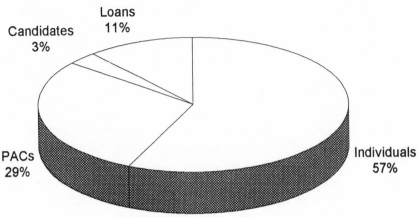

*Source:* FEC press release, March 4, 1993.

Through advanced marketing research and mass mailing techniques candidates can find out what issues concern their constituents, adjust their platforms, and let voters know about these adjustments in further rounds of mail solicitations. Republicans pioneered this approach and maintain their lead over Democrats. In competing with each other for these dollars there is little doubt that both parties have learned a great deal about their constituents' desires.

It appears then that on the demand side contribution limits make it hard for politicians to learn what their constituents want and which interest group pressures to take seriously. In the absence of such information politicians might have to rely on sources which only dimly reflect public concerns. Personal connections could become the way to gain the politician's ear. An extreme example gives some insight. The Third Reich closed democratic channels of communication between rulers and ruled. It came to pass that the way to Adolf Hitler lay through his secretary Martin Bormann. Interest groups had to rely on their past friendship with Bormann or appeal to his greed and whim. In a democracy, contributions cut out middlemen such as Bormann and let groups express the intensity of their preferences directly to the people in charge.

## Supply

Contributing is only one means by which a group can get something from government; lobbying is the other means. Ideally we would like to know how much every interest group spends to influence government in order to examine what fraction is contributions and what fraction is lobbying. This could indicate who would suffer most from a contribution limit. Unfortunately there is no reliable record of how much is spent on all forms of lobbying at the federal level. Anecdotes abound and it is possible that lobby spending is ten times greater than campaign contributions, but there are no systematic data.[4]

There are, however, clues to who relies more on lobbying. As argued earlier, PACs may make contributions to improve a candidate's chances or simply to show him how serious they are about an issue. Often such a group divides its money between both candidates in a race, giving more to incumbents and less to challengers. A group that gives to both sides is probably more interested in signaling its desire to be taken seriously by the winner than in trying to influence the outcome. Corporate and labor PACs are of this sort. They spend only a small fraction of their budgets on advertising for or against a candidate. The biggest part goes directly to candidates in the form of contributions. Nonconnected and health and trade PACs are different. They spend larger fractions of their recorded budgets on grassroots advertising campaigns which they conduct independently of the candidates. Often, as in 1982 and 1986, they spend heavily *against* incumbents. Table 8 shows how independent expenditures by various types of PACs have grown as a fraction of their total budgets.

These patterns of contributing and independent spending are part of larger strategies adopted by the different groups.

Labor and corporate PACs influence policy by making a detailed informed case to those in power. Therefore unions and especially corporations devote a smaller fraction of their resources to direct campaigning and more to contributing (see Table 8).[5] Contributions give these groups the chance to make their cases to politicians. Politicians also need their help. Economic legislation is often difficult to write and subject to piercing intellectual criticism. A study of the Senate found that to deal with these problems senators rely heavily on lobbies

TABLE 8
PAC Contributions to Congressional Campaigns and Independent Spending by PACs in Those Campaigns, 1978–1992 (in thousands of 1992 dollars)

| | Contributions | | | | | | | |
|---|---|---|---|---|---|---|---|---|
| | 1978 | 1980 | 1982 | 1984 | 1986 | 1988 | 1990 | 1992 |
| Corporate | 20,136.5 | 32,201.9 | 39,383.4 | 47,219.4 | 58,255.8 | 58,994.9 | 61,466.7 | 68,252.0 |
| Labor | 20,984.4 | 22,138.8 | 29,072.1 | 32,987.1 | 37,702.4 | 39,602.5 | 36,725.0 | 32,616.0 |
| Nonconnected | 5,299.10 | 8,218.2 | 15,323.7 | 19,286.8 | 23,705.8 | 22,429.7 | 15,934.8 | 18,062.0 |
| Health | 23,739.90 | 26,667.2 | 31,363.5 | 35,514.3 | 41,485.2 | 45,443.6 | 47,375.0 | 53,637.0 |
| Other | 2,119.60 | 3,354.4 | 45,828.0 | 5,054.5 | 6,178.7 | 6,425.2 | 6,747.2 | 7,650.0 |
| Total | 72,279.50 | 92,580.5 | 160,970.7 | 140,062.1 | 167,327.9 | 172,895.9 | 168,248.7 | 180,217.0 |
| Independent expenditures[a] | | | | | | | | |
| Corporate | 26.5 | 27.8 | 256.5 | 904.9 | 19.8 | 26.2 | 17.4 | 47.8 |
| Labor | 30.1 | 27.2 | 36.0 | 30.3 | 38.3 | 73.4 | 149.3 | 298.5 |
| Nonconnected | 273.2 | 374.5 | 347.9 | 1,427.0 | 4,547.4 | 2,361.3 | 2,992.9 | 6,276.7 |
| Health | 191.2 | 948.1 | 1,023.8 | 1,400.2 | 2,698.9 | 1,735.4 | 1,945.9 | 3,422.3 |
| Other | 5.5 | 4.9 | 30.2 | 45.8 | 217.8 | 51.2 | 343.1 | 385.3 |
| Total | 526.5 | 1,382.5 | 1,694.4 | 3,808.2 | 7,522.2 | 4,247.5 | 5,448.76 | 10,430.6 |
| Independent expenditures as a % of PAC independent expenditures plus contributions | | | | | | | | |
| Corporate | 0.13 | 0.09 | 0.65 | 1.88 | 0.03 | 0.04 | 0.03 | 0.07 |
| Labor | 0.14 | 0.12 | 0.12 | 0.09 | 0.10 | 0.18 | 0.40 | 0.91 |
| Nonconnected | 4.90 | 4.36 | 2.22 | 6.89 | 16.10 | 9.52 | 15.81 | 25.79 |
| Health | 0.80 | 3.43 | 3.16 | 3.79 | 6.11 | 3.68 | 3.95 | 6.00 |
| Other | 0.26 | 0.14 | 0.07 | 0.90 | 3.41 | 0.79 | 4.84 | 4.80 |

a. Independent expenditures are monies spent to promote the defeat or election of a candidate or party. PACs cannot coordinate this spending with the candidates.
Sources: FEC press releases; U.S. Department of Commerce. Statistical Abstract of the United States, 1992, 1981 editions; U.S. Department of Commerce, Survey of Current Business, March 1993.

to write their speeches and do office chores. Such help is particularly attractive to members of the party that does not control the White House because they cannot call on the research services of government departments as fully as the other members (Congressional Quarterly Guide, Fall 1991, p. 152).

Even though economic PACs provide valuable services, they do not set policy; "relatively few senators are actually changed by lobbyists from a hostile or neutral position to a friendly one" (Donald R. Matthews quoted in Congressional Quarterly Guide, Fall 1991, p. 152). Lobbyists influence policy by providing legislators with accurate balanced information. As one member of Congress put it, "It doesn't take very long to figure which lobbyists are straightforward, and which ones are trying to snow you. The good ones will give you the weak points as well as the strong points of their case. If anyone ever gives me false or misleading information, that's it—I'll never see him again" (Congressional Quarterly Guide, Fall 1991, p. 152).

The bemused reader may wonder why, if these interest groups have so little influence on legislators, they receive so much government largesse. The example of the defense industry provides an answer. In the 1980s a majority of Americans voted for a larger military. Boeing, Lockheed, General Dynamics, and hundreds of other contractors had little or nothing to do with passing increased defense budgets. But once approved, the budgets had to be spent intelligently. This is where lobbyists came into play, suggesting how the budgeted money should be spent. Each of the large aerospace firms presented well-researched arguments promoting government purchases of its own fighters or missiles. Similarly, broad public support for the environment in the 1980s opened the door for lobbyists to propose sewer projects, waste-site cleanups, solar energy laboratories, pollution control research, park improvements, and fish hatcheries.

To skeptical observers it may appear that the final decision by Congress is influenced by how many people in a defense plant or cleanup program will be employed in a politically sensitive district. Congress manages to turn the public's demand for action into an occasion for porkbarrel politics in which the final allocation of resources has little to do with information carefully provided by lobby groups. Instead, "pork" is directed under the pressure of interest groups to the home districts of powerful members of Congress. How else to explain the many short, haphazard strips of highway built as "special demonstration projects" under the $88 billion highway authorization bill of 1986? The explanation is that such activities can only be carried so far. Congress cannot build strips of highway randomly in order to please the construction industry. The general pattern of highway construction must follow rational principles of traffic science and engineering which benefit many voters (Hird 1991). Pork for the narrow constituencies of special interest groups is constrained by the benefits which the general public receives from well-planned projects. Politicians cannot allow themselves to forget that the popular push behind sensible projects limits their ability to porkbarrel (Becker 1983).

Nonconnected and trade PACs, as opposed to labor and corporate PACs, often promote simpler policy objectives, such as the right to an abortion or the protection of certain professions and trades such as law and medicine. They take their case directly to the public, with their objective often being to unseat or to place candidates. They rely less than other PACs on influencing policy by means of providing detailed information to legislators, so they spend a smaller fraction of their budgets on giving contributions and a greater part on independent spending, as Table 8 shows. Table 9, which summarizes the results of a survey of interest groups in the mid-1980s, shows that only a small fraction of public interest groups contributed directly to candidates' campaigns. These groups were more apt than corporations or labor to publicize incumbents' voting records and run direct-mail campaigns. Buying access through contributions and providing information to candidates are relatively less important to them than putting the pressure of public opinion on a legislator.

These groups can be viewed as middlemen who represent individuals to the politician in much the same way that department stores represent the consumer to the wholesaler. Department stores seek out fine products and bargain with wholesalers for the lowest price. Their bargaining power rests on the allegiance of their many customers. In the same spirit, the public interest group gets power from its individual supporters and invites each candidate to adjust his platform to the group's liking (see Sorauf 1980).

Voters can show how much they care about a variety of issues by giving to various public interest organizations. In roughly the same way that an investor weighs assets in his or her financial portfolio to suit a personal taste for risk and return, a contributor measures out support for various groups and confronts the candidate with a homemade platform or portfolio of preferences. If, for example, I oppose abortion and favor legalization of drugs, I may not find this mix of ideas in any candidate, but I can give money both to the pro-life movement and to the Libertarians in proportion to how strongly I feel on each question. In this way my ideas get freer expression than if I gave directly to the major party candidate roughly closest to my way of thinking.

Contribution limits pose different problems for advocacy and economic PACs. As argued above, advocacy PACs rely more on campaign activities than on lobbying. They try to change election

TABLE 9
Percentage of Lobbying Groups in Each Category Using Various
Lobbying Techniques, 1986

|  | Corporations | Trade associations | Unions | Public interest groups |
|---|---|---|---|---|
| Testifying at hearings | 98 | 100 | 100 | 100 |
| Contacting officials directly | 100 | 97 | 100 | 100 |
| Informal contacts | 98 | 97 | 95 | 96 |
| Presenting research results | 94 | 89 | 90 | 92 |
| Sending letters to members | 85 | 97 | 95 | 86 |
| Entering into coalitions | 96 | 91 | 100 | 92 |
| Shaping implementation of policies | 90 | 91 | 85 | 92 |
| Talking with media | 67 | 89 | 95 | 96 |
| Planning legislative strategy | 81 | 85 | 85 | 83 |
| Helping draft laws | 86 | 94 | 85 | 74 |
| Letter-writing campaigns | 83 | 89 | 100 | 83 |
| Shaping government agenda | 79 | 77 | 85 | 100 |
| Mounting grassroots lobbying | 79 | 80 | 100 | 71 |
| Having constituents contact elected officials | 77 | 94 | 85 | 58 |
| Drafting regulations | 85 | 83 | 75 | 75 |
| Serving on advisory commissions | 74 | 74 | 95 | 67 |
| Alerting members of Congress to effects | 92 | 74 | 85 | 57 |
| Filing suit | 72 | 83 | 95 | 79 |
| Contributing to campaigns | 86 | 66 | 90 | 29 |
| Doing favors for officials | 62 | 56 | 68 | 46 |
| Influencing appointments | 48 | 49 | 80 | 47 |
| Publicizing voting records | 28 | 37 | 90 | 75 |
| Direct-mail fundraising | 19 | 37 | 65 | 75 |
| Running ads in the media | 31 | 31 | 55 | 33 |
| Contributing manpower to campaigns | 14 | 23 | 70 | 33 |
| Endorsing candidates | 8 | 9 | 95 | 25 |
| Engaging in protests | 0 | 3 | 90 | 25 |

Note: There were 52 corporations, 35 trade associations, 20 unions, and 24 public interest groups in the sample.
Source: Schlotzman and Tierney 1986.

outcomes and put pressure on politicians. A contribution limit may leave them with little choice but to spend more on grassroots campaigns, which are not subject to limits, instead of contributing directly to candidates. To run independent campaigns or expand existing operations, advocacy groups must pay setup costs for staff and offices. If there are no limits an advocacy group finding a candidate who is a good match for its beliefs can take advantage of economies of scale in the candidate's organization by simply contributing money. The group's contribution dollar goes further because the candidate has already paid the up-front setup costs of running the campaign. The surge of independent PAC spending that happened after limits were imposed in 1974 is often seen as an encouraging sign of direct citizen action. But it may also reflect a costly expedient forced on advocacy groups by contribution limits.

Economic PACs suffer differently from contribution limits. How are they to show they are serious about an issue if they can only give the candidate $1,000? To gain access to the winner they may turn to other displays of importance such as the establishment of large offices in Washington. Every dollar spent on such displays probably gives the candidate less information about which groups are important than a direct contribution could. Gaining access to candidates becomes more expensive and leaves lobbyists with less money to spend on making an informed case.

The preceding analysis does not mean that all affected groups suffer from contribution limits. As Becker (1983) and others argue, politics is about relative advantage. Contribution limits may restrict all groups, but the group that experiences the least restraint may gain relative to others. The larger loss is the loss of cheap information, as a result of increased setup costs for advocacy groups and access costs for economic lobbies. These problems are currently not extreme, because loopholes let contributors get around the law. But stronger laws such as S3, which would put severe restrictions on soft money, would intensify the effects I have described.

## Legislative Initiatives in the 1990s

The partisan dispute over which party would benefit most from contribution limits has attracted more attention than abstract questions about how the flow of information and the efficient management of government would change. The debate behind the reform proposals of 1992 clearly shows how self-interest shapes the positions Democrats and Republicans take.

Republicans wanted a ban on PAC contributions but not on spending limits. Democrats wanted spending limits on candidates and independent groups, public subsidies, and a ban on PAC contributions. Each side's proposal, if passed into law, would have worked to that side's political advantage. Republicans raise more money than Democrats, but less of it comes from PACs. This is because PACs tend to give more to incumbents, and Republicans are the challenging minority in both houses. Until the early 1980s Republicans did not complain, simply because PACs gave *them* more money. The tide turned against them after they lost control of the Senate in 1986, and by 1989 President Bush was proposing a ban on most types of PACs and an emptying of campaign war chests at the end of each election.

The ban on PAC money might not have hurt Democrats if accompanied by a spending limit. In the end both parties agreed to ban PACs, but for fear of violating the Constitution they inserted a safety clause to the effect that if the Supreme Court found the ban unconstitutional, a milder restriction would take hold: PACs would be allowed to contribute a maximum of $2,500 to a Senate candidate (half the present limit), and the total of such contributions could not come to more than 20 percent of the general election spending limit (between $375,000 and $825,000). For the House, permissible PAC contributions were kept at $5,000, but no candidate could accept more than $200,000 from PACs. S3 would also have made it more difficult to raise soft money and more difficult for an organization to solicit contributions, "bundle" them, and forward them to a candidate.[6]

President Bill Clinton's 1993 proposal built on S3, but added its own innovations. The proposal would not take effect until 1996 and would ban all soft money from federal elections. It would forbid bundling of contributions by corporations, unions, and lobbyists. The president's plan also banned contributions by registered lobbyists to members of Congress whom they had lobbied in the previous year. It set a limit of $2,500 on PAC contributions to Senate candidates. Congressional candidates accepting federal subsidies would face a limit on how much of their private wealth they could spend.[7] As I have explained, the effect of any complicated limits on contributions will be to raise the cost of transmitting political information. President Clinton's plan is no exception.

### Banning Out-of-State Contributions

An issue which has no clear champions in Congress, but about which certain reform groups feel strongly, is whether contributors from out-of-state should obey any special limits. Currently American contributors can give to candidates in any state. Many reformers believe that a candidate should not accept money to serve the interests of any but his own constituents. This opinion makes sense if one does not ponder the reasons behind geographic representation. Attaching a candidate to a narrow district is an efficient way of minimizing the information required for voters to make a sound choice. It only takes a limited number of voters to judge the candidate's character, observing, for example, the extent of involvement in various causes in the community. This valuable information would be hard to gather and advertise at a national level.

Although representatives work for their region, they are also elected to work for the country. If each cared only about his own district there would be no reason for a United States. If contributions send useful messages to candidates, then candidates should be allowed to pay heed to all messages and not simply to the ones from their districts.

There is another reason for out-of-state contributions. Candidates have an incentive to pass expensive spending programs in their districts because the cost can be spread through increased taxation over many districts. If candidates have the security of relying on contributions from out-of-state they will be less vulnerable to this moral hazard. The possibility of out-of-state campaign contributions in local elections "means that the incentive of local politicians to export the cost of local programs will be dampened" (Crain, Tollison, and Leavens 1988).

## Viewing Contributions Rationally

Little good can be said about limiting contributions. Limits weaken communication between politicians and their constituents, raise the cost of elections, and prevent citizens from showing how intensely they feel about issues.

Reformers have argued that we need limits to prevent the unfair political advantage that money can give to tiny groups of people. This argument rests on the shaky and largely unproven assumption that money can buy elections and politicians. It ignores basic facts about the pattern of contributions in society, namely that small individual contributors make up at least half of all political contributions. It also overlooks the many cases where "radical movements . . . have typically been supported by a few wealthy individuals who have become persuaded—by a Frederick Vanderbilt Field, or an Anita McCormick Blaine, or a Corliss Lamont, to mention a few names recently prominent, or by a Friederich Engels, to go farther back. This is a role of inequality of wealth in preserving political freedom that is seldom noted—the role of the patron" (Friedman 1962, p. 17).

---

"Limits weaken communication between politicians and their constituents, raise the cost of elections, and prevent citizens from showing how intensely they feel about issues."

---

Reformers who raise simplistic arguments about "big money" corrupting politicians are out of touch with reality. Voters suffer not from large amounts being spent but from a political monopoly on expression secured by one group. To understand the importance of campaign money we must be aware of the larger context in which spending takes place. As political scientist David Adamany writes:

> Scholarly work on campaign finance tends to concentrate on the amounts spent, the sources from which the money is raised, and the uses to which the money is put. These data are helpful, but they do not show the relationship of campaign finance to the political environment—to the kinds of party systems [and] the available channels of communication. Much less attention is given to money as a form of functional representation than to the very infrequent instances in which campaign gifts are made for the purpose of procuring action by public officials which would have been forthcoming in the absence of contributions (1990).

Focusing only on the amounts spent and contributed narrows our view. Such a focus obscures some of the fascinating devices democracies have come up with for giving ordinary people an important voice in how they are governed. Through a single agent, thousands of citizens can pool many small contributions into a large contribution. Such money reflects popular opinion, and when used to buy advertising it provides the electorate at large with information about issues and candidates. Laws of the sort now in the federal statutes, that limit contributions, make it hard for ordinary people to pool their funds. The administrative burdens that contribution limits impose are particularly hard on new politicians and emerging citizens' groups. This makes limits an important instrument for muting criticism and concentrating the ability to influence elections in the hands of incumbents.

# 7

# *Is Low Voter Turnout a Problem?*

THE MOVEMENT TO LIMIT CAMPAIGN spending is also unwittingly a movement to limit voter turnout. Turnout depends in part on how much candidates spend. Almost all political commentators are concerned about the steep thirty-year decline in the percentage of Americans who vote (see Table 10). But few suggest that more campaign spending could reverse the downward trend. The most commonly proposed solutions are automatic voter registration, government-sponsored voter information programs, and measures such as the creation of government-funded party foundations that would invigorate the parties and return them to their role of the nation's most important political mobilizers. In this chapter I argue that these proposed solutions may increase turnout for a while, but they cannot stop its decline. Nor is it clear that increasing turnout by these means makes for a more informed and enthusiastic electorate.

Unrestricted campaign spending by parties and groups may be the best way to ensure meaningful participation. Campaign spending can provide voters with information and have a lasting effect. Spending alerts voters to the differences between candidates, which gives them a reason to choose between two alternatives. It increases turnout by dispelling the belief that both sides are the same. Any regulation such as a spending or contribution limit that chokes the flow of information will inhibit turnout.

This is not to say that government has no role in promoting turnout, but it must recognize that many of the forces lowering

111

TABLE 10
Percentage Turnout of Those Eligible to Vote
in Presidential Races, 1960–1992

|      | Turnout rate |
|------|--------------|
| 1960 | 62.8 |
| 1964 | 61.9 |
| 1968 | 60.9 |
| 1972 | 55.2 |
| 1976 | 53.5 |
| 1980 | 52.6 |
| 1984 | 53.1 |
| 1988 | 50.2 |
| 1992 | 55.9 |

Sources: FEC press release, January 24, 1993; Ornstein et al., 1992,
p. 48; U.S. Department of Commerce. Statistical Abstract of the
United States, 1989.

turnout are beyond government control. Turnout depends mainly
on education, morals, the number of voters who move frequently,
and the variety of political competition. Changing any one of
these influences is a daunting task. Government's best hope is
to remove awkward barriers to voting, such as complicated
registration procedures, and to find innovative low-cost ways of
letting people vote, such as mail balloting.

The central point of this chapter is that we should not read
too much into so simple an indicator as the percentage who vote.
This type of problem comes up in every public policy field.
Chairmen of the Federal Reserve are plagued with the question
"Is the interest rate too high?" They are at pains to explain that
the interest rate is determined by the demand and supply of
credit, so that when it changes there are many possible interpretations, some good and others bad. The debate on turnout
is no different, and great care must be taken in arguing that
declining turnout is bad. The important question is whether low
turnout affects the quality of candidates serving constituents.
One can imagine a case in which more of the educated vote
while more of those without education stop voting. Overall
turnout would fall, but those choosing candidates would be on
average more informed. One can also imagine fewer people

voting because the consequences of electing either party do not differ greatly. As Alesina and Tabellini have argued, large deficits limit any government's decisions (1990). If it does not matter who gets into power, why vote? And why worry if turnout is low?

This chapter asks these "behind-the-scenes" questions and assesses how worrisome the decline in turnout has been. I suggest that fewer people vote today because the interest groups to which they belong can influence policy merely by threatening to mobilize voters. Advances in communications technology have shifted power away from parties toward interest groups. By reminding politicians of their influence these groups can get results while saving their members the bother of voting. In a roundabout way, the benefits of advances in technology are perhaps passed on to voters who now need to go to the ballot less often.

The first part of the chapter examines why the levels and trends of U.S. turnout differ from those of other countries and tries to interpret the evidence. The second part assesses popular proposals for boosting turnout. I suggest that one of the best ways to do this is to put an end to contribution limits.

## Why Is Turnout Low—and Falling?

The U.S. record on turnout looks bad when viewed against that of other industrialized countries, but it is not clear what this comparison means. Table 11 shows that U.S turnout as a fraction of the voting-age population ranked second-to-last in a sample of twenty countries. Moreover, U.S. turnout has fallen steadily for the past thirty years, as Table 10 shows, while in most other countries it has been stable. These differences may be good or bad depending on the underlying causes.

### The Level

Two common explanations for the low international ranking are that Americans are more alienated from politics and that U.S. political institutions make it harder to vote. Recent evidence throws doubt on the first explanation. Americans are not more cynical and alienated than citizens in other countries. If anything, the reverse is true. Summarizing survey literature, Wolfinger, Glass, and Squire noted that when it comes to pride in political

TABLE 11
Voter Turnout and Institutional Characteristics of Twenty Democracies,
Early 1980s

| | Rank | Average turnout (as % of eligible) | Compulsory voting | Voter registration method |
|---|---|---|---|---|
| Italy | 1 | 94 | yes | automatic |
| Austria | 2 | 88 | no | automatic |
| Belgium | 2 | 88 | yes | automatic |
| Sweden | 2 | 88 | no | automatic |
| Australia | 3 | 86 | yes | those eligible must register |
| Denmark | 4 | 85 | no | automatic |
| W. Germany | 4 | 85 | no | automatic |
| New Zealand | 5 | 83 | no | those eligible must register |
| Finland | 6 | 82 | no | automatic |
| Netherlands | 6 | 82 | no | automatic |
| Norway | 6 | 82 | no | automatic |
| Israel | 7 | 80 | no | automatic |
| France | 8 | 78 | no | voluntary |
| Spain | 8 | 78 | no | automatic |
| Ireland | 9 | 77 | no | automatic |
| U.K. | 10 | 75 | no | automatic |
| Japan | 11 | 72 | no | automatic |
| Canada | 12 | 68 | no | automatic |
| U.S.A. | 13 | 54 | no | voluntary |
| Switzerland | 14 | 44 | no | automatic |

Source: Adapted from Powell 1986.

institutions, Americans ranked first in a study of countries including Italy, West Germany, and the United Kingdom (1990). The number of Americans who claimed to be "interested in politics" was 48 percent, highest in an eight-country sample. The number who claimed to be active in politics was 24 percent in the same study, also highest. Another survey found that only 16 percent of Americans felt there was nothing they could do about an unfair proposal under consideration by government. The corresponding numbers were 10 percent for West Germany and 13 percent for Switzerland, but 25 percent for the United Kingdom, 44 percent for Finland, and 56 percent for Austria. Americans' belief in the political efficacy of the individual ranked second highest out of ten countries. Their belief in government responsiveness ranked second highest in another survey of nine countries. In short, psychological attitudes cannot explain the relatively low turnout in the United States.

There is agreement among voting scholars that the single most important reason for the difference in participation rates between the United States and other democracies is the difficulty of registering to vote (Powell 1986, Wolfinger, Glass, and Squire 1990). Among the Western democracies only the United States requires citizens to take the initiative both to register and to vote (with the possible exception of France). In Australia, Belgium, Greece, Italy, and Spain citizens are required by law to vote. In most other countries voter registration is automatic in the sense that the government maintains records of each citizen's name and address or that registration is conducted by officials who go door-to-door before each election.

---

"I suggest that fewer people vote today because the interest groups to which they belong can influence policy merely by threatening to mobilize voters."

---

These examples suggest that if it were easier to register, more Americans would vote. This could be accomplished by allowing registration closer to the day of election (most states require registration thirty days before the election), by keeping longer hours at registration offices, and by purging election rolls less frequently. The "Motor Voter" bill proposed by President Bill Clinton is another example of what can be done to increase turnout. The bill would require states to allow citizens to register at motor vehicle offices and offices that provide such public assistance as welfare and unemployment compensation checks. The bill would also require states to institute uniform procedures for registration by mail.

Americans get very little help in voter registration from their parties. As Teixeira explains, in other democracies "political parties actively attempt to engage citizens in the electoral process, thereby taking a considerable amount of the burden of voting off the shoulders of the individual. . . . In the United States, the state plays almost no role, and the parties comparatively little in mobilizing the voter into the electoral arena" (1987, p. 122).

Powell summarized the effect of the above forces in a sample of industrialized democracies and found that political attitudes, such as beliefs about government efficacy and responsiveness, add 5 percent to U.S. turnout but the party system and other institutional factors reduce turnout by 13 percent and registration procedures reduce it further by 14 percent (1986).

## The Trend

These comparisons may explain why the *level* of turnout is lower in the United States, but they only hint at why the *trend* is down. We need to see what is causing the trend in order to decide whether it is alarming. The two most likely forces at work are a change in the makeup of American voters and the decline of parties. Understanding these forces can help us see low U.S. turnout in an optimistic light.

Education is the darling of voter-turnout enthusiasts because people who have more of it vote more often. It comes as a shock to notice that turnout has been falling as more people have taken high school and university degrees. Teixeira (1987) looked for other changes in the makeup of voters that could explain the trend during the period from 1960 to 1980. He noted that the young, those who drift between communities, and the unmarried and divorced vote less and that their number increased in the period he studied. Teixeira showed that "increased educational attainment . . . acted to push turnout upward. . . . But, at the same time, the proportions of the electorate that were young, residentially mobile, and single increased, acting to depress turnout levels. The effects of these two sets of changes were of the same magnitude, so the net impact of demographic change on turnout was negligible" (p. 107). The movement of these demographic variables is shown in Table 12.

Building on the work of Shaffer (1981) and Abramson and Aldrich (1982), Teixeira went on to find that 88 percent of the turnout decline between 1960 and 1980 could be explained by people losing allegiance to their parties. One sign of decreasing party allegiance is an increase in "ticket splitting" (that is, voting for a presidential candidate from one party and congressional

TABLE 12
Voter Characteristics and Turnout, 1960–1980
(percentage of those eligible who voted)

|      | 12 or more years of education | Aged 37 or older | Single | Moved in past 2 years | Strongly partisan |
|------|------|------|------|------|------|
| 1960 | 51.4% | 69.0% | 20.0% | 25.4% | 36.3% |
| 1964 | 55.2% | 68.0% | 23.0% | 26.5% | 38.1% |
| 1968 | 59.6% | 69.0% | 29.0% | 28.0% | 29.9% |
| 1972 | 62.5% | 62.0% | 33.0% | 29.6% | 23.8% |
| 1976 | 69.6% | 59.0% | 37.0% | 31.3% | 23.3% |
| 1980 | 74.2% | 58.0% | 39.0% | 33.2% | 26.4% |

Source: Adapted from Teixeira 1987, p. 17.

candidates from another). Ticket splitting between presidential and House races rose from 14 percent in 1960 to 38 percent in 1980 (Wattenberg 1990). Voters who split their tickets make their choices according to the quality of the candidate more than the party they belong to and are less likely to listen to any party's message to get out and vote.

As Americans lost allegiance to their parties they became more closely attached to interest groups. Some indication of this trend is shown in Table 13 (adapted from Wattenberg, p. 158), which tracks the rise in the proportion of those who feel they are part of a social group. What is not immediately clear is why moving from a party to an interest group would stop members from wishing to vote. The reason may involve the fact that many interest groups pay minor attention to election campaigns, instead exercising much of their influence by lobbying. If citizens believe that their group is lobbying well they may see little need to vote. This theory, however, cannot be the whole story.

### The Silver Lining

There may be also a more subtle effect at work which can help us answer whether declining turnout is a bad thing. If politicians adjust their platforms in *anticipation* of group protests, then groups have no need to send their members to the polls. Sometimes a group will mobilize voters if it is competing directly with another group. The battle between pro-choice and pro-life activists is a good example. But in most cases a group faces no

TABLE 13
Social Groups with Which Voters Identify, 1972–1984
(in percentages)

|  | 1972 | 1976 | 1980 | 1984 |
|---|---|---|---|---|
| Middle class | 52.1 | 65.8 | 65.4 | 77.3 |
| Workers | 42.1 | 55.5 | 62.9 | 72.9 |
| Young | 43.7 | 48.7 | 51.4 | 61.9 |
| Elderly | 40.7 | 50.8 | 57.0 | 59.0 |
| All whites | 39.2 | 46.0 | 46.5 | 62.2 |
| Women | 33.1 | 44.6 | 41.7 | 58.7 |
| Farmers | 26.3 | 32.9 | 40.5 | 46.9 |
| Poor | 25.2 | 32.6 | 41.5 | 46.9 |
| Business | 16.3 | 19.7 | 28.4 | 43.5 |
| Southern whites | 15.0 | 18.4 | 19.9 | 26.8 |
| Blacks | 14.6 | 12.9 | 18.4 | 27.6 |

Source: Adapted from Wattenberg 1990, p. 158.

organized opposition and need only remind politicians of its ability to mobilize voters in order to influence policy. Much of the power of these groups has come from advances in communication technology which lower the costs of setting up and running a political operation. Groups have in turn passed these savings on to voters by relieving them of the need to vote in every election. Low voter turnout is perhaps a sign that voters are choosing their leaders at less personal cost. Those who vote are increasingly educated (see Table 12) and interested in politics. The growing proportion of such demanding people has probably done much to make campaigns more informative.

## Turnout and Campaign Spending

High or low turnout can be the result of varied factors. In Italy turnout stands at 94 percent, but the bizarre practice of sometimes posting the names of nonvoters outside the town hall or stamping "DID NOT VOTE FOR FIVE YEARS" on identification papers probably does no more than encourage public cynicism (Seton-Watson 1983). Switzerland has the lowest turnout on the chart of industrialized nations, but its people are known for their exceptional civic spirit. In the United States low voter turnout cannot be a symptom of apathy or lack of political interest. In survey after survey Americans outshine almost every other country in political interest. The hypothesis has not been fully tested, but it is possible that Americans turn out in smaller numbers because they have less need to do so, not because of dysfunctional "societal disincentives to turnout" (*Elections '88,* 1989c, p. 143). There is no logical reason why everybody's energy should be mobilized to the fullest during elections. Low turnout may reflect an efficiently organized political system in which people are called to vote by their groups only if they need to. Americans may also feel that groups who represent them can do so effectively by lobbying the government, no matter which party rules.

On occasion groups and parties will need to get their supporters to the polls and in these moments of need it is important that they be able to do so. Campaign funds help do this. Caldeira and Patterson (1982) have found that "Campaigning can mobilize an electorate when partisan strengths are aroused, elections are hotly contested, outcomes are in doubt, and voters are activated by . . . advertising, media appearances by candidates, canvassing, drives to get out the vote, and the like." Matsusaka and I have found that the same holds true for Canadian elections and that people tend to vote more when they have more information (1992a, 1992b).

Spending conveys information that lets people see the differences between the candidates. The greater these differences appear, the more reason people will have to vote. A less obvious benefit of campaign spending may be its cumulative effect. Kristian Palda was the first to show that advertising for commercial products created a "stock" of goodwill that could last years (1963). Similarly, campaign advertising may leave citizens with the sense that politics are worth paying attention to and participating in. This sense may last for years and contribute to turnout for years.

### Voter Information Programs

The effect of contribution and spending limits on turnout depends on how these limits are applied. If limits cover only candidates, interest groups might take up the slack. If they apply to all, as many in Congress would wish, then turnout could fall. This might not daunt supporters of these limits if government paid for voter information programs. Many such programs exist in state elections, and it is important to ask whether they can take up the task that campaign spending does.

In a study commissioned by the House of Representatives, the General Accounting Office (GAO) found that:

> Contrary to widely held beliefs, voter information activities do not generally increase voter turnout. . . . Information campaigns that educate voters about registration deadlines, registration drives, and places and hours of registration did not significantly increase the turnout of states having long intervals between the last day of registration and the day of election. . . . States consistently target low-voting populations—such as youths, minorities, and women—in their voter information campaigns but . . . these campaigns seem to have little effect in increasing overall turnout (1990, p. 57).

Some states spent as much as $1 million on their programs "but whatever the amount it seems to have little bearing on turnout. For example, Minnesota, the state with the highest turnout in 1988, spent only $5,000 on voter information activities, while Hawaii and the District of Columbia, a state and a district with very low turnouts, spent $503,906 and $121,200 respectively" (U.S. General Accounting Office 1990, p. 57). The study found a few exceptions. For example, states that mailed information about propositions and referendums to households had higher voter turnout than states that did not.

---

"Government does not know enough about information potential voters need. By spending money on voter information programs it is providing a service no one demands."

---

The GAO did not speculate on why all those millions of state taxpayer dollars seemed to have no effect on turnout, but the discussion in the present chapter hints at an answer. Government does not know enough about information potential voters need.

By spending money on voter information programs it is providing a service no one demands. Private groups are much more in tune with what motivates their members. The remarkable success of Jesse Jackson's 1984 voter registration drive shows that minorities are not resistant to information, provided it is from a source they trust on a matter that interests them. Jackson's campaign and other liberal groups raised $7 million to get the poor, the unemployed, blacks, and other minorities registered. Black turnout rose by five percentage points above the 1980 level (*Elections '88,* 1989c, p. 143).

### What Should Be Done

It may not be possible or even desirable to reverse the trend of turnout, but the state could temporarily change the level. The General Accounting Office has come strongly to the conclusion that registration procedures are an important factor in low turnout. Most political scientists hold this opinion and would agree with Wolfinger that "registration is more difficult than voting. It often requires more obscure information and a longer journey at a less convenient time. Registration deadlines pass quietly and the experience usually is a solitary one [but] once Americans are registered, they are very likely indeed to vote in presidential elections. About 85 percent of National Election Study respondents whose registration was verified actually voted in each of the three presidential elections of the 1980's" (1992, pp. 22–23).

The GAO found that registration deadlines well in advance of the election accompanied lower turnout and that "all mail ballot elections in selected elections led to a twenty- to forty-percentage point increase in turnout, with a cost that was at least 32 percent lower on a per ballot basis than the cost of conducting conventional polling place elections" (1990, p. 41). It recommended a toll-free number which people could call to learn if they had been purged from election rolls, and it proposed an experiment to test the feasibility of letting people mail in their votes for Congress and the president. The GAO's recommendations support the main government turnout initiative of the 1980s, the National Voter Registration Act of 1989. This law was passed by the House but not by the Senate. It would have obliged states to include a voter registration section in the application form for a driver's license and to make it easier to mail in one's registration. President Bill Clinton revived this initiative in early 1993.

### What Should Not Be Done

Plans to make registration easier are constructive because they spare voters the disincentive of dealing with government red tape. But other more sophisticated recommendations for boosting turnout, such as candidate subsidies, government money for party foundations, and last-minute opinion-poll blackouts can do harm.

Many believe that publishing last-minute opinion polls can discourage turnout. A voter who sees which party is ahead or behind in the polls may think it is not worth the trouble to vote. To stop this disintegration of morale, the argument goes, government should ban publication of opinion polls for several days before an election. This may indeed boost turnout but at the cost of fostering ignorance about an important trend. If a party leaps ahead in the polls at the last moment, the knowledge may remove from some the moral obligation of voting, benefiting the elderly and anyone else who finds it costly or inconvenient to travel to the polls. Last-minute knowledge also lets voters act strategically. In 1980 34 percent of Americans split their tickets between presidential and House races. A popular reason for ticket splitting is to keep a balance of power between the president and Congress. This is an example of strategic voting. If I see that one party will fill both offices I may decide to split my ticket. Without last-minute information I might make the wrong choice.

---

"What matters is that voters make informed choices at low cost and that people believe the electoral system gives them a say."

---

There is some evidence that subsidies to parties can increase turnout. In Germany parties receive approximately DM 500 million to promote voter education and participation (Bertram 1992, p. 9). In 1983 the average turnout in the German federal election was 89.1 percent, one of the highest rates among industrialized democracies. Does the subsidy lead to a more informed choice of candidates? Can this result be achieved without a subsidy? There is as yet no solid ground for the optimism of subsidy enthusiasts. In other democracies subsidies distort elections by giving large parties an advantage.

## Some Conclusions about Turnout

High voter turnout should not necessarily be a goal of campaign finance regulation. What matters is that voters make informed choices at low cost and that people believe the electoral system gives them a say. Even though U.S. turnout is low in comparison with that of other countries, Americans are among the people most interested in and enthusiastic about politics. Another positive sign is that the educated are an increasing percentage of those who vote.

Low American turnout may reflect the beneficial effects that interest groups have on elections. The power they wield can convince politicians to adopt their policies. This allows voters to influence policy without showing up to vote in great numbers. In a sense interest groups do the work for those eligible to vote. Turnout may have fallen since 1960 in part because of the rise of such groups.

Government can help voters by making it easier for voters to register, by making registration automatic, and by allowing people to vote through the mail. Government should not ban last-minute election polls, because they give voters potentially useful information. Nor should parties receive public subsidies to boost turnout. It is not clear that such subsidies will lead to more informed voter choices. Neither should government impose spending limits. Limits reduce what voters know about their candidates and may reduce turnout. Under spending limits turnout may fall, and those who go to the polls may be less informed.

# 8

# *Political Competition and the Public Interest*

THE AIM OF THIS BOOK is to ask what effect campaign finance laws have on political competition and to explain how constituents can profit from political competition. Many reformers believe that spending and contribution limits would keep millionaires and well-funded incumbents from dominating politics. They also believe that campaign subsidies would allow politicians to spend more time thinking up intelligent policies and less time bowing to the needs of special interest groups. I have argued that, on the contrary, spending limits, contribution limits, and subsidies can entrench incumbent candidates and lessen political competition. Election laws are the rules of the game which incumbents may write in their own favor.

To see why these laws may not be in the public interest, it is important to understand how information flows between candidates and voters. One of the main differences between democracies and dictatorships lies in who controls the truth. Dictatorships give the ruling party a monopoly on advertising. Democracies scatter the right to advertise. This allows all concerned to criticize government for bad decisions. Transmitting information is an important way of holding politicians accountable.

Most voters do not have the ability or interest to keep close track of their leaders. They must wait until the election and rely on the free information derived from political advertising. Specialized interest groups and challenging politicians provide this information. They make it their job to dispute the government's version of the facts. Every advance in communications technology makes it cheaper for small independent groups and obscure challengers to learn what voters want and to send voters their message. Because many groups have a chance to compete, no single group dominates policy by very much or for very long. Neither can incumbents indulge their own views of policy unless these views are in line with what voters want. These benefits of free debate are weakened by laws that interfere with the flow of information or give one group a monopoly on advertising.

These points are not widely recognized, perhaps because of deep prejudices many people have concerning the role of money in elections. What has not been made clear in the debate on electoral reform is that money alone does not buy elections. What can buy elections is a monopoly on campaign spending. Spending limits go part of the way toward giving incumbents such a monopoly. It is essential to look at the kinds of regulations under which spending takes place. How useful campaign spending is to voters can depend on these regulations. To truly understand the role of election money in a democracy we must be sensitive to this regulatory background, and we must question the crude caricatures that some reformers use to support their views.

In challenging these caricatures, a growing number of academics have tried to measure the dangers of limits, subsidies, and other campaign regulations such as complicated registration procedures and expense-reporting requirements. Their studies have found that incumbent spending is two or three times less potent at winning votes than challenger spending. This happens because incumbents campaign continuously during their term of office. They have franking privileges, paid professional staff, and travel allowances which they can use to promote themselves and build a block of devoted supporters. By the time of the election there is little that campaign money can do for them. Spending limits protect the advantage which incumbents have built up against attacks by fresh challengers. Subsidies spare incumbents the need to raise money and may cut them off from the demands of their constituents. Contribution limits and complicated registration procedures are an additional barrier to newcomers because such regulations make it very expensive to run an informative campaign. Much of what challengers spend goes simply to administrative overheads instead of toward reaching voters. Estimates for congressional and presidential races put the costs of complying with complicated regulations at roughly 10 percent of what is spent on a campaign.

Congressional incumbents have not yet been able to pass the restrictive measures that incumbents in other Western democracies take for granted, but this is not for lack of trying. For the past twenty years Congress has taken advantage of political scandals, such as Watergate in 1974 and the House banking scandal of 1992, to pass bills that limited spending by politicians and outlawed advertising by private American citizens and groups. Only presidential vetoes and the Supreme Court's defense of free speech have prevented these bills from becoming law. But as Democratic senator David Boren warned after the defeat of S3, the 1992 campaign finance law, "We'll be back."

---

"Campaign finance law cannot be a magic bullet. It will not stop government from growing or corruption from spreading."

---

What Congress has managed to do is to limit the size of contributions. This has forced politicians and independent citizens to look for small contributions in many places. It has also hindered large coalitions of concerned citizens from pooling their resources and making their opinions heard. When members of Congress complain that they spend too much time trying to raise money, they are complaining about a problem of their own creation. Contribution limits have also led to wasteful searches for ways to stretch the law. It is expensive for presidential candidates to educate their fundraisers about the legal perils of raising soft money. Moreover, soft money is not as effective as ordinary contributions because candidates can spend it only on a very narrow aspect of the campaign. Such a constraint reduces the effect that money can have on an election.

One particularly unpleasant tendency of Congress has been to make it hard for new parties and private citizens to participate in elections. Presidential subsidies are geared toward Republicans and Democrats. Newcomers must satisfy burdensome conditions before getting their presidential or congressional candidates on the ballot. Congress has repeatedly tried to outlaw what private citizens can spend to promote their views during a campaign. A common theme among incumbents from the main parties is that they need protection against "unbalanced" criticism from "unaccountable" citizens groups. Fortunately, U.S. incumbents have not had the same luck in muting free speech as their counterparts in Canada, France, Great Britain, and Germany— countries where the established parties have a near monopoly on election-time speech.

If, as I have argued here, there are dangers in allowing incumbents to regulate themselves, what can we expect of campaign finance laws? Campaign finance law cannot be a magic bullet. It will not stop government from growing or corruption from spreading. If groups are not allowed to advertise they will shift their energies to lobbying. Such a shift in effort will work to the advantage of politicians and interest groups who prefer to conduct their business in private, away from public debate.

Good campaign laws allow candidates to learn the desires of the electorate and allow the electorate to exercise an informed choice. Election law should keep registration requirements simple and should restrain incumbents from using government resources to promote themselves. There is little room in good campaign law for limits on contributions and spending or for any other rule that reduces the amount of information available to voters.

# Notes

Chapter 1 is not annotated.

**Chapter 2**

1. A few years later Pinto-Duschinsky found no evidence of rising costs in parliamentary elections in Britain (1981). Central party spending was much lower in 1979 than in 1964, and "despite comments about the Conservatives' use of 'modern' media techniques, the party spent no more, in real terms, on centrally funded publicity than it had half a century earlier in 1929" (p. 236). This is a significant observation because parties do most of the spending in British elections. Candidates spend very little.

2. Such a calculation for presidential elections after 1972 would be meaningless because since then presidential campaigns have been subject to a fixed real spending limit.

3. The FCC survey shows that many stations violated the spirit of a 1972 law directing broadcasters to charge candidates "the lowest unit charge of the station" that commercial advertisers pay for "the same class and amount of time for the same period" (Alston 1991, p. 138).

4. There is no cheap airtime provision for the House because of that chamber's much lesser dependence on broadcasting.

5. In 1959 Congress amended the Federal Communications Act to include the Fairness Doctrine. A U.S. Court of Appeals ruled in 1986 that the congressional amendment did not have the force of law but was more like a directive giving the Federal Communications Commission (FCC) permission to write and enforce a Fairness Doctrine. Under the leadership of Marc Fowler, a Reagan appointee, the FCC moved to abolish the doctrine, but in 1987 Congress voted that the FCC could not do this. President Reagan vetoed Congress and denounced the doctrine as "antagonistic to the freedom of expression guaranteed [by the constitution]" (Ranney 1990, p. 198).

6. See Rosen (1986) for a good discussion of Tournament Theory, a theory which asks how the efforts of contestants in win-lose contests will vary with the size of the prize and the skill of the players.

7. See Magelby and Nelson (1990), Nugent and Johannes (1990).

8. See also the FEC *Campaign Guide for Nonconnected Committees, Campaign Guide for Corporations and Labor Organizations,* and *Campaign Guide for Political Party Committees.*

## Chapter 3

1. Senate Resolution 3 would have given senators broadcast vouchers for advertisements of between one and five minutes but not for quick sound bites of thirty seconds.

2. Content analysis is an academic branch of sociology and journalism which breaks news stories or advertisements into types of statements. The frequency of each type is a formal measure of the message's content (see Miljan 1992).

3. See Wittman (1989, p. 1407) for a counterexample, however.

4. Spending is not a sign of public endorsement when it comes from the candidate's personal wealth, but it may still carry information. By using his own fortune a candidate shows that he is confident enough of his own integrity and ability to invest in himself. The founders of new companies often invest heavily in their own enterprises to convince outside investors to buy equity. According to Myers and Majluf, the expression of commitment despite risk is what makes personal spending a credible signal (1984).

5. Spending limits foster a climate in which politicians and special interests can strike deals undisturbed by angry publicity. In such a climate the returns to lobbying are greater, and perversely, even though a limit could decrease what is spent on a campaign, a limit may actually *increase* the amount of money society spends on political activity because special interests lobby more (a costly activity) due to the increased returns (see Nelson 1976). In India and Turkey, where it is very costly to advertise against political misdeeds, Krueger has estimated that up to 7 percent of gross national product is wasted by lobbyists in their pursuit of government protection and quotas (1974). This pursuit is possible in part because incumbents are less exposed to public opinion in those countries and have greater leeway to deal with special interests. The returns to successful lobbying are therefore greater and more effort is expended on what Tullock has called "rent-seeking" (1980).

## Chapter 4

1. Further supporting evidence can be found in the work of Glantz, Abramowitz, and Burkart (1976), Abramowitz and Segal (1986), and Thomas (1989).

2. Caution must be exercised before concluding that limits always hurt challengers. Other factors, such as the ability to raise money and the level of the limits, can figure heavily in the result. To illustrate, suppose that the incumbent can raise $100,000 and receives 1 vote per dollar, while the challenger can raise $75,000 and receives 2 votes per dollar. If a ceiling of $50,000 is imposed, it does not affect the chances of either candidate. The incumbent suffers twice the loss in money-raising power, but that money is only half as potent in his hands as in the

challenger's hands. The ceiling would cost him votes if his money-raising power were any greater and gain votes if it were lower.

3. Also see Jacobson (1985), Palda and Palda (1985, 1992).

4. Other reasons for the rise in retirements in 1992 were: (1) redistricting, which pushed members with previously safe seats into new, hostile districts, (2) a rise in congressional pensions, and (3) 1992 was the last year members could retire and keep unspent campaign funds for personal use (Katz 1992).

5. It is not known how widely candidates use office staff to help them campaign. The answer is probably "Not much." A large part of the growth in congressional staff in recent years is due to increases in constituent casework. Large staffs can, however, provide candidates with important information on what sorts of policies constituents will favor.

6. In 1991 a Royal Commission on election procedure and finances, headed by representatives of the three established parties, recommended that spending by independent groups should be allowed but in the limited amount of $1,000 per group, per election. It was hoped that this minuscule gesture would make the law appear constitutional.

7. See the volume by Nugent and Johannes (1990) for a full statement of this view.

8. For a survey of loopholes see Bedelington (1990).

## Chapter 5

1. Revenues from the tax checkoff have fallen off in recent years, and the Federal Election Commission has expressed concern that in the near future there may be too little money in the fund to fully subsidize the federal presidential contests.

2. In addition, each state has a different spending limit. For example, New Hampshire, the first and perhaps most important primary in the nation, allows a primary contestant to spend only $500,000. Adding to the complexity is the fact that the sum of the spending limits of all the states is roughly three times the candidate's overall primary spending limit.

3. The precise formula is $4 million multiplied by the ratio of the minor party's presidential vote in the previous election to the average of the vote received by the major party candidates in the previous election.

4. The formula is the same as in the previous endnote.

5. Only certain types of bank loans are not counted (U.S.C. 431[8][B][vii]). In particular, those on which the bank charges its regular rate of interest for the category involved and that are made on a basis that assures repayment are not counted as contributions. Finding a bank to do business in this way may be harder than finding private investors because the candidate who wishes to borrow against future reimbursement is borrowing against future votes. Banks have little expertise in assessing the risks involved, and this may make it too costly for the candidate to borrow from them.

6. To avoid the complication of discussing a three-dimensional graph, I have put both challenger and incumbent spending on the same axis. This creates the conceptual problem that if both candidates' expenditures

are rising at the same time on the same axis, both their votes cannot be rising, since they are fishing from the same pond of voters. However, the main point of the example is that challenger spending may only appear productive because the challenger spends little relative to the incumbent. If the incumbent is a better candidate, then equal spending brought about by subsidies would not help the challenger to win. The same point can be made more precisely in three dimensions, but for brevity I have taken this less exact route in my exposition.

Please also note that this simple example assumes that subsidy money is just as effective a winner of votes as are campaign contributions. As I warned in Chapter 4, money alone does not buy votes. The way the money was raised is important. A thousand dollars raised in small amounts from individuals may win more votes than $1,000 in subsidy because it reflects broad popular support. The point to keep in mind for Figure 7 is that subsidies may not be able to equalize the chances of challengers and incumbents.

**Chapter 6**

1. See Mueller (1989) for a partial survey of this huge field of research.

2. Sometimes such access can be troublingly close, as in the case of the Keating Five which spanned the late 1980s. Charles H. Keating, Jr., a savings and loan operator, engaged the help of five members of Congress in a battle he was having against federal regulators. Senator Alan Cranston took an especially active role on Keating's behalf, and Keating raised $994,000 in campaign resources for Cranston over the 1980s. A Senate ethics committee gave Senator Cranston a reprimand.

3. See Frank Sorauf's excellent 1992 book, which puts the power of PACs in reasonable perspective.

4. Some systematic evidence comes from Canada, but it is difficult to know how closely it applies to the United States. In surveys of lobby groups Stanbury found that roughly ten times as much was spent on lobbying in the years of his survey than on campaign contributions (1978).

5. Labor unions make intensive use of almost all types of lobbying strategy, so they are not altogether similar to corporations, which rely mainly on contributions to influence policy.

6. Bundling is a way of getting around contribution limits. An individual contributor can give his contribution to a middleman and designate or earmark that contribution for a specific candidate or committee. The middleman can collect these contributions without limit and present them to a candidate.

7. Under the Clinton proposal House candidates who accepted public subsidies could not accept more than $200,000 from PACs, $200,000 in individual contributions greater than $200, and the remainder from individual contributions less than $200. Senate candidates who took federal subsidies could not spend their own private wealth in sums greater than the lesser of $250,000 or 10 percent of the general election spending limit. For House candidates the limit is $50,000.

Chapter 7 is not annotated.

Chapter 8 is not annotated.

# References

## General Sources

Abramowitz, Alan I. 1988. "Explaining Senate Election Outcomes." *American Political Science Review* 82 (June): 385–403.

———. 1991. "Incumbency, Campaign Spending, and the Decline of Competition in U.S. House Elections." *Journal of Politics* 53:34–56.

Abramowitz, Alan I., and Segal, Jeffrey A. 1986. "Determinants of the Outcomes of U.S. Senate Elections." *Journal of Politics* 48:433–39.

Abrams, Burton A., and Settle, Russell F. 1978. "The Economic Theory of Regulation and the Public Financing of Presidential Elections." *Journal of Political Economy* 86 (April): 245–57.

Abramson, Paul, and Aldrich, John. 1982. "The Decline of Electoral Participation in America." *American Political Science Review* 76:502–21.

Adamany, David. 1969. *Financing Politics: Recent Wisconsin Elections.* Madison: University of Wisconsin Press.

———. 1990. "The Unaccountability of Political Money." In *Money, Elections, and Democracy: Reforming Congressional Campaign Finance,* edited by Margaret Latus Nugent and John R. Johannes, pp. 95–116. San Francisco: Westview Press.

Alesina, Alberto, and Tabellini, Guido. 1990. "Voting on the Budget Deficit." *American Economic Review* 80:37–49.

Alexander, Herbert E. 1984. *Financing Politics.* Washington, D.C.: Congressional Quarterly Press.

———. 1989. "Money and Politics: Rethinking a Conceptual Framework." In *Comparative Political Finance in the 1980s,* edited by Herbert E. Alexander and Joel Federman, pp. 9–23. Cambridge: Cambridge University Press.

———. 1991. "The Regulation of Election Finance in the United States and Proposals for Reform." In *Comparative Issues in Party and Election Finance,* edited by F. Leslie Seidle, pp. 3–56. Toronto: Dundurn Press.

Alexander, Herbert E., and Bauer, Monica. 1991. *Financing the 1988 Election.* San Francisco: Westview Press.

Alexander, Herbert E., and Haggerty, Brian A. 1981. *The Federal Election Campaign Act: After a Decade of Political Reform.* Washington, D.C.: Citizens' Research Foundation.

——. 1987. *Financing the 1984 Election.* Lexington, Ky.: Lexington Books.

Alston, Chuck. 1991. "Forcing Down Cost of TV Ads Appeals to Both Parties." *Congressional Quarterly Guide to Current American Government,* Fall, pp. 135–39.

——. 1992. "Campaign Finance Bills Compared." *Congressional Quarterly Weekly Report,* February 29, pp. 489–94.

Becker, Gary S. 1958. "Competition and Democracy." *Journal of Law and Economics* 1:105–9.

——. 1983. "A Theory of Competition Among Interest Groups for Political Influence." *Quarterly Journal of Economics* 98 (August): 371–400.

Bedelington, Anne H. 1990. "Loopholes and Abuses." In *Money, Elections, and Democracy: Reforming Congressional Campaign Finance,* edited by Margaret Latus Nugent and John R. Johannes, pp. 69–94. San Francisco: Westview Press.

Bender, Bruce. 1988. "An Analysis of Congressional Voting cn Legislation Limiting Congressional Campaign Expenditures." *Journal of Political Economy* 96:1005–21.

Bennet, W. Lance. 1977. "The Ritualistic and Pragmatic Bases of Political Campaign Discourse." *Quarterly Journal of Speech* 63:38–57.

Bertram, Eric. 1992. "Comparative Studies in Electoral Reform and Party Finance: The Federal Republic of Germany." In *Comparative Research Notes on Electoral Reform and Party Finance,* edited by F. L. Seidle, pp. 1–34. Ottawa: Royal Commission on Electoral Reform and Party Financing.

Budde, Bernadette A. 1980. "Business Political Action Committees." In *Parties, Interest Groups, and Campaign Finance Laws,* edited by Michael J. Malbin, pp. 9–25. Washington, D.C.: American Enterprise Institute.

Caldeira, Gregory A., and Patterson, Samuel C. 1982. "Contextual Influences on Participation in U.S. State Legislative Elections." *Legislative Studies Quarterly* 7:359–81.

"Campaign Finance Reform." 1992. *Congressional Digest* 71 (March): 67–77.

Campaign Finance Study Group. 1979. Introductory chapter in U.S. Congress. House of Representatives. Committe on House Administration. *An Analysis of the Impact of the Federal Election Campaign Act, 1972–1978.* From the Institute of Politics, Kennedy School of Politics, Harvard University. Washington, D.C.: U.S. Government Printing Office.

Carter, John R., and Racine, Robert A., Jr. 1990. "Relative Campaign Spending and House Elections, 1982–1988." Working paper, College of the Holy Cross, Worcester, Mass.

Cheney, Richard B. 1980. "The Law's Impact on Presidential and Congressional Election Campaigns." In *Parties, Interest Groups, and Campaign Finance Laws,* edited by Michael J. Malbin, pp. 238–53. Washington, D.C.: American Enterprise Institute.

Cloud, David S. 1988. "Senate Declines New Approach to Limiting Campaign Finances." *Congressional Quarterly Weekly Report,* April 23, p. 1108.

Cobb, Jean. 1988. "The Power of the Purse." *Common Cause Magazine,* May/June, pp. 13–18.

Congressional Quarterly Guide to Current American Government. 1988. "Pork: A Time-Honored Tradition Lives On." Fall, pp. 67–74.

———. 1990. "The Maze of Spending Limits: An Election Field Guide." Fall, pp. 8–13.

———. 1991a. "Most House Members Survive, But Many Margins Narrow." Spring, pp. 3–5.

———. 1991b. "The Washington Lobby." Fall, pp. 149–53.

Cook, Rhodes. 1991. "Incumbents' National Status Breeds Local Distrust." *Congressional Quarterly Weekly Report,* February 23, pp. 141–45.

Crain, Mark W., Tollison, Robert D., and Leavens, Donald R. 1988. "Laissez-faire in Campaigning Finance." *Public Choice* 56: 201–12.

Crete, Jean. 1991. "Television, Advertising and Canadian Elections." In *Media and Voters in Canadian Election Campaigns,* edited by Frederick J. Fletcher, pp. 3–44. Toronto: Dundurn Press.

Donovan, Beth. 1992. "Overhaul of Election Funding Unlikely to Become Law." *Congressional Quarterly Weekly Report,* April 11, p. 931.

*Elections '88.* 1989a. "The Business of Politics." Pp. 132–38. Washington, D.C.: Congressional Quarterly Inc.

———. 1989b. "The Campaign Finance Debate." Pp. 119–26. Washington, D.C.: Congressional Quarterly Inc.

———. 1989c. "Why America Doesn't Vote." Pp. 139–47. Washington, D.C.: Congressional Quarterly Inc.

Epstein, Edwin M. 1980. "Business and Labor Under the Federal Election Campaign Act of 1971." In *Parties, Interest Groups, and Campaign Finance Laws,* edited by Michael J. Malbin, pp. 107–51. Washington, D.C.: American Enterprise Institute.

Faber, Ronald J., and Storey, M. Claire. 1984. "Recall of Information from Political Advertising." *Journal of Advertising* 13:39–44.

Ferejohn, John A. 1977. "On the Decline of Competition in Congressional Elections." *American Review of Political Science* 71:166–76.

Ford, Gary T., Smith, Darlene B., and Swasy, John L. 1990. "Consumer Scepticism of Advertising Claims: Testing Hypotheses from the Economics of Information." *Journal of Consumer Research* 16:433–41.

Franzitch, Stephen E. 1982. *Computers in Congress: The Politics of Information.* Beverley Hills: Sage Publications.

Friedman, Milton. 1962. *Capitalism and Freedom.* Chicago: Chicago University Press.

Germond, Jack, and Witcover, Jules. 1985. *Wake Us When It's Over: Presidential Politics of 1984.* New York: Macmillan.

Glantz, Stanton A., Abramowitz, Alan I., and Burkart, Michael P. 1976. "Election Outcomes: Whose Money Matters?" *Journal of Politics* 38:1033–38.

Hayek, Friederich H. 1945. "The Use of Knowledge in Society." *American Economic Review* 35:519–30.

Hird, John A. 1991. "The Political Economy of Pork: Project Selection at the U.S. Army Corps of Engineers." *American Political Science Review* 85:429–56.

Horry, Isabella, Palda, Filip, and Walker, Michael M. 1992. *Tax Facts Eight*. Vancouver: Fraser Institute.

Howard, Anthony. 1976. "Political Parties and Public Funds." *New Statesman*, September, pp. 295–96.

Husted, Thomas A., Kenny, Lawrence W., and Morton, Rebecca B. 1991. "Campaign Expenditures and Voter Information: Evidence on the Malfeasance of Elected Officials." Working paper, University of Florida, Department of Economics.

———. 1992. "Evidence on the Truthfulness of the Campaign Information Provided about Incumbent Legislators." Working paper, University of Florida, Department of Economics.

Jacobson, Gary C. 1978. "The Effects of Electoral Campaign Spending in Congressional Elections." *American Political Science Review* 72:469–91.

———. 1979. "Public Funds for Congressional Campaigns: Who Would Benefit?" In *Political Finance*, edited by Herbert E. Alexander, pp. 99–127. London: Sage Publications.

———. 1985. "Money and Votes Reconsidered: Congressional Elections 1972–1982." *Public Choice* 47:7–62.

Johnston, R. J. 1978. "Campaign Spending and Votes: A Reconsideration." *Public Choice* 33:83–92.

———. 1987. *Money and Votes: Constituency Campaign Spending and Election Results*. New York: Methuen.

Joslyn, Richard A. 1980. "The Content of Political Spot Ads." *Journalism Quarterly* 57 (Spring): 92–98.

Katz, Jeffrey L. 1992. "Record Rate of Retirements Suggests Major Shakeup." *Congressional Quarterly Weekly Report*, April 4, pp. 851–55.

Krueger, Anne O. 1974. "The Political Economy of the Rent-Seeking Society." *American Economic Review* 64:291–303.

Leoni, Bruno. 1991. *Freedom and the Law.* Indianapolis: Liberty Fund.

Lott, John R., Jr. 1989. "Explaining Challengers' Campaign Expenditures: The Importance of Sunk Nontransferable Brand Name." *Public Finance Quarterly* 17 (January): 108–18.

Lucas, Robert E., Jr. 1972. "Expectations and the Neutrality of Money." *Journal of Economic Theory* 4:103–24.

Magelby, David B., and Nelson, Candice J. 1990. *The Money Chase: Congressional Campaign Finance Reform*. Washington, D.C.: The Brookings Institution.

Mansfield, Michael W., and Hale, Katherine. 1986. "Uses and Perceptions of Political Television: An Application of Q-Technique." In *New Perspectives on Political Advertising*, edited by L. L. Kaid, Dan Nimmo, and Keith R. Sanders, pp. 268–92. Carbondale: Southern Illinois Press.

Matsusaka, John G., and Palda, Filip. 1992a. "The Downsian Voter Meets the Ecological Fallacy." *Public Choice.*

———. 1992b. "Voter Turnout: A Horse Race." Working paper, University of Southern California School of Business.

McAllister, Ian. 1985. "Campaign Activities and Electoral Outcomes in Britain: 1979 and 1983." *Public Opinion Quarterly* 49:489–503.

McKelvey, Richard D., and Ordershook, Peter C. 1984. "Rational Expectations in Elections: Some Experimental Results Based on a Multi-dimensional Model." *Public Choice* 44:61–102.

———. 1985. "Elections with Limited Information: A Fulfilled Expectations Model Using Contemporaneous Poll and Endorsement Data as Information Sources." *Journal of Economic Theory* 36:55–85.

McNeill, William H. 1963. *The Rise of the West: A History of the Human Community.* Chicago: University of Chicago Press.

Miljan, Lydia A. 1992. "The Methodology and Procedures of the National Media Archive." *Canadian Journal of Communications* 17:95–116.

Montgomery, Peter. 1989. "Funny Money." *Common Cause Magazine,* May/June, pp. 29–31.

Moore, Walter K. 1980. "The Case of an Independent Political Action Committee." In *Parties, Interest Groups, and Campaign Finance Laws,* edited by Michael J. Malbin, pp. 56–67. Washington D.C.: American Enterprise Institute.

Mueller, Dennis C. 1989. *Public Choice II.* Cambridge: Cambridge University Press.

Myers, Stewart C., and Majluf, Nicholas S. 1984. "Corporate Financing and Investment Decisions When Firms Have Information That Investors Do Not Have." *Journal of Financial Economics* 13:187–221.

Nelson, Candice. 1990. "Loose Cannons: Independent Expenditures." In *Money, Elections, and Democracy: Reforming Congressional Campaign Finance,* edited by Margaret Latus Nugent and John R. Johannes, pp. 47–68. San Francisco: Westview Press.

Nelson, Phillip. 1976. "Political Information." *Journal of Law and Economics* 19:315–36.

Novak, Viveca, and Cobb, Jean. 1987. "The Kindness of Strangers." *Common Cause Magazine,* September/October, pp. 32–37.

Nugent, Margaret Latus, and Johannes, John R. 1990. *Money, Elections, and Democracy: Reforming Congressional Campaign Finance.* San Francisco: Westview Press.

Ornstein, Norman J., Mann, Thomas E., and Malbin, Michael J. 1992. *Vital Statistics on Congress 1991–1992.* Washington, D.C.: American Enterprise Institute.

Orren, G. R. 1979. "The Impact of the Federal Election Campaign Act: The View from the Campaigns." In U.S. Congress. House of Representatives. Committee on House Administration. *An Analysis of the Impact of the Federal Election Campaign Act, 1972–1978.* From the Institute of Politics, Kennedy School of Politics, Harvard University. Washington D.C.: U.S. Government Printing Office.

Palda, Filip. 1989. "Electoral Spending." Ph.D. dissertation, University of Chicago.

——. 1991. *Election Finance Regulation in Canada: A Critical Review.* Vancouver: Fraser Institute.

——. 1992. "The Determinants of Campaign Spending: The Role of the Government Jackpot." *Economic Inquiry* 30 (October): 627–38.

Palda, Kristian S. 1963. *The Measurement of Cumulative Advertising Effects.* Englewood Cliffs, N.J.: Prentice-Hall.

——. 1973. "'Does Advertising Influence Votes?' An Analysis of the 1966 and 1970 Quebec Elections." *Canadian Journal of Political Science* 6:638–55.

——. 1975. "The Effect of Expenditure on Political Success." *Journal of Law and Economics* 18:745–71.

Palda, Filip, and Palda, Kristian S. 1985. "Ceilings on Campaign Spending: Hypothesis and Partial Test with Canadian Data." *Public Choice* 45:313–31.

——. 1992. "Campaign Spending and Campaign Finance Issues: An Economic View." *Journal des Economistes et des Etudes Humaines* 3:291–314.

Paltiel, Khayyam Zev. 1979. "The Impact of Election Expenses Regulation in Canada, Western Europe, and Israel." In *Political Finance,* edited by Herbert E. Alexander, pp. 15–39. London: Sage Publications.

——. 1980. "Public Financing Abroad: Contrasts and Effects." In *Parties, Interest Groups, and Campaign Finance Laws,* edited by Michael J. Malbin, pp. 354–70. Washington, D.C.: American Enterprise Institute.

——. 1981. "Campaign Finance: Contrasting Finances and Reforms." In *Democracy at the Polls: A Comparative Study of Competitive National Elections,* edited by Howard R. Penniman, pp. 138–72. Washington, D.C.: American Enterprise Institute.

Panitch, Leo. 1977. "The Role and Nature of the Canadian State." In *The Canadian State: Political Economy and Political Power,* edited by Leo Panitch, pp. 3–27. Toronto: University of Toronto Press.

Patterson, Thomas W., and McLure, Robert D. 1976. "Television and the Less-Interested Voter: The Costs of an Informed Electorate." *Annals of the American Academy of Political and Social Science* 425:88–97.

Patton, Gary W. R., and Smith, Bruce. 1980. "The Effects of Taking Issue Positions on Ratings of Political Candidates." *Political Psychology* 2:20–34.

Peck, Louis. 1990. "Campaign Financing." *Congressional Quarterly* Issue Brief No. 101–9.

Pinto-Duschinsky, Michael. 1981. "Financing the British General Election of 1979." In *Britain at the Polls, 1979: A Study of the General Election,* edited by Howard R. Penniman, pp. 210–40. Washington, D.C.: American Enterprise Institute.

Powell, G. Bingham, Jr. 1980. "Voting Turnout in Thirty Democracies: Partisan, Legal, and Socio-Economic Influences." In *Electoral Participation: A Comparative Analysis,* edited by Richard Rose, pp. 5–34. Beverly Hills: Sage.

——. 1986. "American Turnout in Comparative Perspective." *American Political Science Review* 80:17–43.

Ranney, Austin. 1990. "Broadcasting, Narrowcasting, and Politics." In *The New American Political System,* edited by Anthony King, pp. 175–201. Washington, D.C.: American Enterprise Institute.

Riordan, Theresa. 1987. "Who's Campaigning?" *Common Cause Magazine*, May/June, pp. 12–19.

Rosen, B., and Einhorn, H. J. 1972. "Attractiveness of the 'Middle of the Road.'" *Journal of Applied Psychology* 2:157–65.

Rosen, Sherwin. 1986. "Prizes and Incentives in Elimination Tournaments." *American Economic Review* 76:701–16.

Rothschild, Michael L. 1974. "The Effects of Political Advertising on the Voting Behavior of a Low Involvement Electorate." Ph.D. dissertation, Stanford University, California.

———. 1978. "Political Advertising: A Neglected Policy Issue in Marketing." *Journal of Marketing Research,* 15:58–71.

Rudd, Robert. 1989. "Effects of Issue Specificity, Ambiguity on Evaluations of Candidate Image." *Journalism Quarterly* 66:675–82.

Sabato, Larry J. 1985. *PAC Power: Inside the World of Political Action Committees.* New York: W. W. Norton.

———. 1987. "Real and Imagined Corruption in Campaign Financing." In *Elections American Style,* edited by A. James Reichley, pp. 155–79. Washington, D.C.: The Brookings Institution.

———. 1989. *Paying for Elections: The Campaign Finance Thicket.* Washington, D.C.: Twentieth Century Fund.

Schlotzman, Kay L., and Tierney, John T. 1986. *Organized Interests and American Democracy.* New York: Harper and Row.

Seton-Watson, Christopher. 1983. "Italy." In *Democracy and Elections: Electoral Systems and Their Political Consequences,* edited by Vernon Bogdaner and David Butler, pp. 110–81. Cambridge: Cambridge University Press.

Shaffer, Robert. 1981. "A Multivariate Explanation of Decreasing Turnout in Presidential Elections, 1960–1976." *American Journal of Political Science* 25:68–95.

Smith, Hedrick. 1988. *The Power Game: How Washington Works.* New York: Random House.

Snyder, James M., Jr. 1990. "Campaign Contributions as Investments: The U.S. House of Representatives, 1980–1986." *Journal of Political Economy* 98:1195–1227.

Sorauf, Frank J. 1980. "Political Parties and Political Action Committees: Two Life-Cycles." *Arizona Law Review* 22:445–63.

———. 1992. *Inside Campaign Finance: Myths and Realities.* New Haven: Yale University Press.

Stanbury, William T. 1978. "Lobbying and Interest Group Representation in the Legislative Process." In *The Legislative Process in Canada: The Need for Reform,* edited by W.A.W. Neilson and J. C. MacPherson, pp. 167–207. Toronto, Institute for Research on Public Policy.

Stigler, George J. 1971. "The Theory of Economic Regulation." *Bell Journal of Economics and Management Science* 2:3–21.

Teixeira, Ruy A. 1987. *Why Americans Don't Vote: Turnout Decline in the United States 1960–1980.* New York: Greenwood Press.

——. 1992. ". . . What If We Held An Election and Everybody Came?" *The American Enterprise,* July–August, pp. 50–59.

Thomas, Scott J. 1989. "Do Incumbent Campaign Expenditures Matter?" *Journal of Politics* 51 (November): 965–76.

Tullock, G. 1980. "Efficient Rent-Seeking." In *Toward a Theory of the Rent-Seeking Society,* edited by James B. Buchanan, Robert D. Tollison, and Gordon Tullock, pp. 97–112. College Station, Texas: Texas A&M University Press.

Twentieth Century Fund Task Force on Political Action Committees. 1984. *What Price PACs?* New York: Twentieth Century Fund.

Wattenberg, Martin P. 1990. "From a Partisan to a Candidate-centered Electorate." In *The American Political System: Second Version,* edited by Anthony King, pp. 139–74. Washington, D.C.: American Enterprise Institute.

Wertheimer, Fred. 1991. "After Senate Victory Campaign Finance Battle Shifts to House of Representatives—And White House." *Common Cause Magazine,* July/August, pp. 43–45.

Winter, Ralph K., Jr. (in association with John R. Bolton). 1973. "Campaign Financing and Political Freedom." Washington, D.C.: Domestic Affairs Studies of the American Enterprise Institute, No. 19.

Wittman, Donald. 1989. "Why Democracies Produce Efficient Results." *Journal of Political Economy* 97:1395–1424.

Wolfinger, Raymond E. 1992. "The Rational Voter Faces Election Day: What Your Rational Choice Theorist Won't Tell You about American Elections." Unpublished manuscript, University of California at Berkeley.

Wolfinger, Raymond E., Glass, David P., and Squire, Peverill. 1990. "Predictors of Electoral Turnout: An International Comparison." *Policy Studies Review* 9:551–74.

Wolfinger, Raymond E., and Rosenstone, Steven J. 1980. *Who Votes?* New Haven, Conn.: Yale University Press.

## U.S. Government Publications

Federal Election Commission. 1985. *Campaign Guide for Nonconnected Committees* (June).

——. 1988. *Campaign Guide for Congressional Candidates and Committees* (July).

——. 1989. *Campaign Guide for Political Party Committees* (September).

——. 1990. *Federal Election Campaign Laws* (October).

——. 1992a. *Federal Code of Regulations: Federal Elections* 11 (January).

——. 1992b. *Campaign Guide for Corporations and Labor Organizations* (March).

U.S. Congress. House of Representatives. 1992. *Congressional Campaign Spending Limit and Election Reform Act of 1992.* Conference Report 102–487 to Accompany S3, 102d Cong., 2d sess.

U.S. Congress. Senate. 1988. *Joint Resolution Proposing an Amendment to the Constitution of the United States Relative to Contributions and Expenditures Intended to Affect Congressional and Presidential Elections.* S.J. Res. 282, 100th Cong., 2d sess.

———. 1991. *Joint Resolution Proposing an Amendment to the Constitution of the United States Relative to Contributions and Expenditures Intended to Affect Congressional and Presidential Elections.* S.J. Res. 35, 102d Cong., 2d sess.

U.S. Department of Commerce. 1978. *Statistical Abstract of the United States,* 98th Edition.

———. 1980. *Statistical Abstract of the United States,* 100th Edition.

———. 1981. *Statistical Abstract of the United States,* 101st Edition.

———. 1986. *Statistical Abstract of the United States,* 106th Edition.

———. 1989a. *Statistical Abstract of the United States.* 109th Edition.

———. 1989b. *Survey of Current Business* (August).

———. 1991. *Statistical Abstract of the United States,* 111th Edition.

———. 1992. *Statistical Abstract of the United States,* 112th Edition.

U.S. General Accounting Office. 1990. *Voting: Some Procedural Changes and Informational Activities Could Increase Voter Turnout* (November).

# Court Cases

*Richard H. Austin, Michigan Secretary of State and Frank J. Kelley, Michigan Attorney General v. Michigan Chamber of Commerce,* 110 S. Ct. 1391 (1990).

*James L. Buckley et al. v. Francis R. Valeo, Secretary of the United States Senate,* 424 U.S. 1 (1976).

*Federal Election Commission v. Massachusetts Citizens for Life, Inc.,* 479 U.S. 238 (1986).

*Federal Election Commission v. National Conservative Political Action Committee et al.,* 470 U.S. 480 (1985).

*Federal Election Commission et al. v. National Right to Work Committee et al.,* 459 U.S. 197 (1982).

*First National Bank of Boston et. al v. Bellotti, Attorney General of Massachusetts,* 435 U.S. 765 (1978).

# About the Author

Filip Palda is Senior Economist at the Fraser Institute in Vancouver. He received his B.A. and his M.A. in economics from Queen's University, Kingston, Ontario, and in 1989 he earned a Ph.D. in economics from the University of Chicago. His dissertation, "Electoral Spending," was directed by Nobel laureate Gary S. Becker. From 1989 to 1991 Dr. Palda was a professor of economics at the University of Ottawa. He has published two books, *Election Finance Regulation in Canada: A Critical Review* and *Tax Facts Eight*, and has published numerous articles on the theory and measurement of political phenomena. He writes a syndicated column for the Sterling chain of newspapers and appears regularly in the media as an economic commentator.